# Looking Back

### at the

# Cariboo-Chilcotin

### with

# Irene Stangoe

## HERITAGE HOUSE

CANADIAN CATALOGUING IN PUBLICATION DATA

Stangoe, Irene, 1918-
Looking back at the Cariboo-Chilcotin with Irene Stangoe

ISBN 1-895811-25-2

1. Cariboo Region (B.C.)–Biography.
2. Chilcotin River Region (B.C.)–Biography.
3. Frontier and pioneer life–British Columbia Cariboo Region.
4. Frontier and pioneer life–British Columbia–Chilcotin River Region.
I. Title.
FC3845.C3Z48 1997    971.1'7503'0922    C97-910138-7
F1089.C3S72 1997

First Edition 1997

Heritage House wishes to acknowledge the support of Heritage Canada, the British Columbia Arts Council and the Cultural Services Branch of the Ministry of Small Business, Tourism and Culture.

In addition, we encourage our readership to support the B.C. Archives and Records Service (BCARS) and other institutions acknowledged on our photo credits. They help make publications such as this possible.

Front Cover and Chapter Heading Photos: Chris Schmidt, Alexis Creek
Back Cover Photo (Springhouse Ranch): Angie Mindus
Photo of Author: Doug Layman, Ladysmith
Cover, Book Design and Typesetting: Darlene Nickull
Editor: Antonia Banyard

HERITAGE HOUSE PUBLISHING COMPANY LTD.
Unit #8 - 17921 55th Ave., Surrey, BC V3S 6C4

Printed in Canada by Friesens

## Dedication

This one's for Elaine and Ward

## In Appreciation

Again, my thanks to Cariboo Press, the *Williams Lake Tribune* and publisher Gary Crosina for the use of *Tribune* files, and particularly to photographer Angie Mindus and production manager Gaylene Desautels, for their cheerful and patient help with photographs.

I am also deeply indebted to all those who shared their memories and historical information with me, and trusted me with their treasured photos of bygone days: Rhona Armes, Winnie Gavelin, Terry Crosina, Mike Isnardy, Alice Tresierra, Lon Godfrey, Veasy Collier, Molly Forbes, Sonia Cornwall, Dru Hodgson, Iris Blair, Margaret Gilbert, Barb Poirier, Rudy Johnson, Melva Kinvig, Chuck Wiggins, Don Robertson, Bill O'Donovan, Edna Jacobson, Bob Shaw, Bill Barlee, Ilma Dunn, Barbara Buckley, Don Sale, and Dave Falconer.

Special thanks to local historian John Roberts who has always been most generous in allowing me access to his extensive files on Cariboo-Chilcotin history, and in loaning me photographs.

And of course as always to my husband Clive for his constant encouragement.

My appreciation also to the Cultural Services Branch, Ministry of Small Business, Tourism and Culture for B.C. Their grant was of great assistance in the research and writing of this book.

---

Although the word Indian is in disfavour these days with some First Nations leaders and other authorities, I have chosen to retain use of this traditional, time-honoured name when referring to the Cariboo-Chilcotin's first inhabitants in the historical context of these stories. B.C. photo credits have been assigned when identifiable.

Irene Stangoe

# Table of Contents

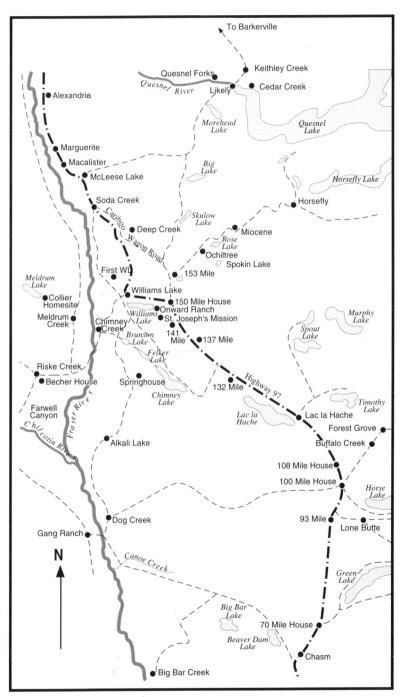

**The Central Cariboo-Chilcotin**

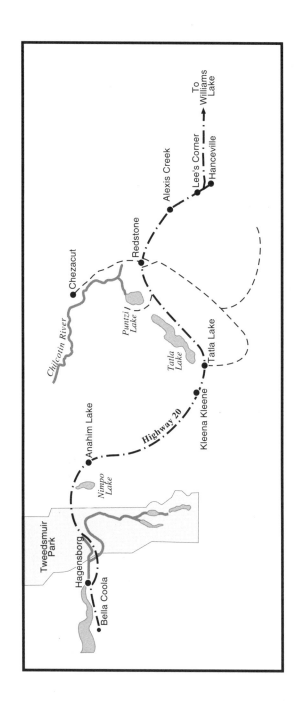

**The Central Cariboo-Chilcotin**

## Looking Back with Irene

"Renovate? RENOVATE?? You're out of your mind, woman," bellowed local historian Alf Bayne who was also Williams Lake's only dentist.

We stood facing one another belligerently in the tiny *Tribune* office. The year was 1950.

"American tourists would drive hundreds of miles to see something like this," the angry dentist continued. I stared with disbelief at the old splintery wood floor, the flyspecked brown walls and the rusty wood heater which Clive and I had acquired along with the newspaper, the *Williams Lake Tribune*, earlier that year.

"But, Alf," I spluttered defensively, "I have to WORK in this."

Sadly he left our historic office, mumbling "No one has a sense of history any more. Women!"

It was the coldest winter on record when I travelled up to the Cariboo via the Pacific Great Eastern Railway to join my editor husband in February. I remember looking out at the awesome Fraser Canyon bathed in frigid moonlight as I cuddled down in my berth, thankful for the potbellied stove which warmed the wooden coach, and the dim light from the swaying old fashioned lamps.

I didn't know then that the "Please Go Easy" had a reputation for occasionally losing a train here and there, and I slept blissfully unaware that slides had blocked the rails several times during the night. It took thirty hours to get from Squamish to Williams Lake, and it was 45 below when I arrived at Williams Lake, having warmed up from a shuddering 54 below. (Would you believe it was 72 below at Exeter Station near Lac la Hache?)

There was ice on the windowsills *inside* our tiny apartment over the newspaper plant, and frost formed on the walls as we struggled to heat the uninsulated rooms with a sawdust burner stove and one small oil heater, and stuffed toilet paper around the single paned windows to try and stop the icy air from creeping in.

We lived there six years, freezing in winters, roasting in summer. We patched up the holes in the masonite walls, tried to squeeze our worldly goods into two small cupboards, tried to ignore the inch-thick dust which sifted in from the unpaved streets in summer, and tried to remember not to flush the toilet too often (it overflowed the septic tank in the backyard and triggered a frightful outcry from our back shop staff of 2 1/2 people).

1951

Somehow we even found room for the two children who came along. "That's the way to bring them up," boomed Lillooet publisher and good friend Margaret "Ma" Murray one night as Ward and Elaine slept peacefully through the din of a cattle sale party.

Why not? They had been brought up on the steady thump, thump, thump of the old Country Brower press downstairs as it pounded hour after hour, grinding out the weekly *Tribune* two pages at a time. "How do you stand the noise?" visitors often asked. And I truthfully answered, "What noise?"

Up until 1950, a newspaper was something I read in the evening and used to wrap the garbage the next morning. But then it became something I laughed and cried over and worked impossible hours to create. Faced with deadlines I learned to do impossible things, and had some of the most fascinating and most shattering experiences imaginable.

One of the first incidents occurred on a day early in 1950 when I was alone in the *Tribune* office. The door burst open and a local businessman stood in front of me trembling with the violence of his emotions, his face white with anger.

"I'm going to sue," he spit out the words one by one. It was over an innocuous reference to his store in an anonymous letter to the editor, if I remember correctly, but I was scared silly. I was new to the game and apprehensive over every misplaced comma, so I had visions of Clive's dream, a newspaper of his own, vanishing with the printing of those few short words. Luckily it didn't happen.

For two years running we goofed on Daylight Saving Time and told our readers to put their clocks back when it should have been ahead, and the following year were a whole day out! We hunkered in our apartment the following Sunday, wondering how many people would be late? early? for church, and died a thousand deaths.

*Clive Stangoe became the youngest newspaper publisher in B.C. in 1950 and ran* The Tribune *for twenty-three years. Irene contributed social and history articles for over four decades. The couple lived in the upstairs apartment of this original building on Oliver Street. (*Williams Lake Tribune *photo)*

It was on a day in 1950 that Maple Leaf Hotel owner Benny Abbott sang the whole chorus of "Good-night Irene" to me as we stood before the teller's window at the Bank of Montreal, and the red of my face matched our bank statement. It could only happen in the Cariboo.

The year 1950 was also the only time we missed a deadline. Jim Stitt, our back shop foreman, went on holiday and Clive was left to struggle with our temperamental, antiquated linotype which I swear was held together with baling wire and chewing gum.

Thursday's deadline came and went, then Friday's. Subscribers phoned, came to the office, and stopped us as we slunk down the street. By Saturday the editor had bags under his eyes from the sleepless nights, but still struggled valiantly on. At one o'clock in the morning even I got into the battle and discovered what Jim did when he stood on the little platform at the back of the linotype, and fed little squares of metal called "matrices" into the &!*$^# machine.

Sunday was definitely not a day of rest, and Clive laboured on in the dingy cobwebbed back shop, attempting to find out even more about the innards of a linotype. When Jim came back to work Monday morning and asked brightly, "How did the paper go?" we had to admit sadly that we didn't know. It still wasn't out.

Those were the days when we had to "stuff" the newspaper by hand; that is, insert the pages into one another. It was a backbreaking, time-consuming job which had to be slogged through until the mountainous stacks of pages were reduced to neat piles of completed newspapers. John Gibbon, our halftime student worker, was a whiz at it. He could put those pages together faster than anyone in the shop and although I tried and tried, I could never beat him.

*Employee, Jim Stitt (right) works the old linotype in the back room while Claude Middlestead (left) uses the old Brower press to print two pages at a time. (*Williams Lake Tribune *photos)*

I never dreamed during those hectic first years that this was a historic time in the newspaper game and that the pounding press, the linotype, and the hand-set type would soon be things of the past. Who could imagine the *Tribune* would one day be produced on a massive offset press capable of printing and folding thousands of copies a hour; that the back shop would be a bright room full of computerized equipment operated by a couple of petite gals in jeans or miniskirts; or that reporters would sit glued to computers in the quiet newsroom tapping out copy to be transferred by electronic wizardry into printed stories ready for "paste up." Although technology has changed and despite the marvellous things that can be accomplished with computers, the newspaper business will never be able to completely eliminate the goofs that appear in the written word.

I had written nothing more exciting than a high school essay before, but in 1950 I became the *Tribune's* social editor (among other things) and for years suffered through an incredible number of horrible "typos" that somehow seemed to creep into my wedding write-ups.

I became quite philosophical about minor mistakes such as the bride carrying *moses* instead of roses, and *bowels* of carnations decorating the bridal table, and these would produce only low moaning sounds of anguish. But when I became hysterical, the editor knew that something tragic had happened. Like the time the wedding couple in question exchanged *cows* at the altar; yes, COWS, not vows.

Someone sent that charming little "bon mot" to Wilf Bennett at the *Vancouver Province* and he commented in his "Good Morning" column that "I know Williams Lake is the biggest cattle-shipping point in the province, but even I was surprised to find they were exchanging cows at weddings."

Clive's classic typo story revolves around a special event in the Roman Catholic church in which we reported–on the front page yet–that "Holy Mess" was celebrated. We only twigged to the mistake when a subscriber came in to gleefully scoop up twenty copies. He wasn't an RC but his wife was.

But despite the dust and deadlines, they were happy years in a small friendly town where everybody knew everybody else and we never locked our doors; when keeping cows off the main street was one of the village commission's most pressing problems, and raising the price of haircuts from 75 to 85 cents was front page news.

Wonderful, marvellous memories to look back on some forty years later, to remember the people I met and interviewed, particularly the pioneers who helped shape this country, and to be able to pass along some of their history.

As a historical note, the *Tribune* was established in 1930 by William Percy Cotton who sold it to Chilcotin rancher George Renner in 1937. We purchased the newspaper from Renner in 1950, sold to Northwest Publications in 1966 (with Clive remaining on as publisher) but bought it back three years later in partnership with Alan Black. In 1973 the Black family assumed full ownership. As well as the *Tribune*, the Black Press now owns 80 community newspapers and ten regional press plants throughout B.C., Alberta and Washington State making it the largest privately held newspaper group in Canada.

*Clive Stangoe, proofs copy in his tiny office under the stairs at the* Tribune. *Notice the indispensable paste-pot, scissors and old Underwood typewriter.* (Williams Lake Tribune *photo*)

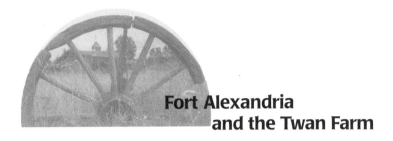

# Fort Alexandria
## and the Twan Farm

Dave Twan was just a lad of fifteen when he helped his dad, John Sanford Twan, tear down the old Hudson's Bay Fort on the family ranch at Fort Alexandria on the west side of the Fraser River in 1922. His dad felt pretty bad about having to destroy the historic structure, but he just couldn't find anyone interested in preserving it. "He had anchors and cables holding it up," Dave told me, "but it had already started to lean badly. If it had ever come down, it could have killed stock housed in a barn nearby or some of our family."

The old fort was just a shell by that time, of course, badly in need of a new roof and foundation. As soon as the cables were cut, it almost fell down of its own accord.

Dave and his dad used a crosscut saw to cut up the old timbers, but it wasn't easy. Broken arrowheads buried in the wood—reminders of the Chilcotins who periodically attempted raids on the fort—played havoc with the saw, and the huge timbers of dry hard fir, a foot thick, were difficult to saw through.

Dave remembered the crumbling fort as a tall building which appeared to be ingeniously constructed, in sections eight to ten feet long with a four by six inch loophole every eight feet for guarding against Indian attacks. The structure needed very few nails, just a few square ones. The massive horizontal timbers had been stacked one by one into deep four-inch grooves hacked out by an axe down the length of the vertical timbers tying the structure together. "I have never seen another like it," Dave said.

His dad also found an old musket with a four-foot barrel, a relic from the fort. The lead pellets had to be tamped down with wadding. "It must have taken a long time to load up and shoot again," Dave chuckled, remembering how he and his brothers used to swipe the lead pellets because "they were great to play with."

According to Quesnel historian Louis LeBourdais, an underground passage led at one time from the fort to a storehouse which had a powder magazine beneath the surface. This was to prevent a surprise attack on the powder and food supplies.

But this building was not the first Fort Alexandria. The original one, named for Alexander Mackenzie, was established by the North West Company in 1814 on the east side of the Fraser, about twenty miles north of Soda Creek. This is believed to be the farthest point south reached by the famed explorer in 1793 in his search for an outlet to the Pacific.

In 1821 the North West Company amalgamated with the Hudson's Bay Company and that year a new HBC fort was built some miles further north. It was abandoned in 1837, and a third one (eventually owned by the Twans) was built on the west side of the river to better trade with the Chilcotins. Incidentally, the original name was probably "Fort Alexander," but later got changed to "Alexandria."

To give you some idea of the importance of Fort Alexandria, try to imagine the interior of the province, called New Caledonia then, peopled only by Indian villages and the big isolated log forts like Fort Kamloops, Fort George, and Fort Fraser. Manned by a large staff of clerks, traders, canoe men, trappers, interpreters, and labourers, they were the only pockets of civilization throughout the vast wilderness.

As a transhipment centre, Fort Alexandria was one of the largest and most important of these forts. As soon as the ice went out on the northern lakes and rivers, the voyageurs began their epic journey south with fur-laden canoes. At Fort Alexandria several hundred pack horses waited to transport the furs south to Fort Okanogan in central Washington state, and from there they went by canoe again following

*Dave went north to Fort George on the* BX, *with its famous flat-bottom hull shown here under construction at Soda Creek in 1910. The* BX *design included a splash cover for the 21-foot-wide sternwheel allowing a comfortable view from the aft ladies' cabin. (Vancouver Public Library photo) When the Twan family went to Fort George they passed through the dangerous Fort George Canyon where Dave's beloved* BX *eventually grounded itself while hauling 100 tons of cement downstream. (BCARS photos)*

the Columbia River to Fort Vancouver (now Vancouver, Washington). There the furs were loaded onto ships for the final leg to the lucrative London markets.

On the return journey the voyageurs loaded up with trade goods to exchange with the Indians for their furs. The colourful striped HBC blankets and a scarlet flannel cloth loved by native women were among the most popular items.

Although Fort Alexandria was a busy place during the summer, with natives camped outside its log walls and many people coming and going, winter was another matter. Life at the fort became dreary and monotonous, and the food often poor, with the men subsisting mainly on dried salmon with fresh game or the odd horse or dog thrown in for variety if nothing else was available.

By the late 1850s, however, the end was in sight for Fort Alexandria. When gold was discovered on the lower Fraser River, a wave of eager men poured up the fur brigade trails into the Interior in their search for the motherlode. In an effort to capitalize on this new business, the HBC built a store on the east side of the Fraser lessening the importance of Fort Alexandria.

But the Cariboo Wagon Road, built in 1862-5 to give access to the rich finds at Barkerville, was the final nail in Fort Alexandria's coffin, so to speak. Stopping houses and small settlements sprang up along its length, offering food, lodging and goods, so trade declined drastically at both the store and the fort. Fort Alexandria on the west bank of the Fraser, inaccessible except by boat, was particularly hard hit and closed permanently in 1867.

John Twan, Dave's father, obtained a Crown grant in the late 1800s which included the abandoned fort. He established his ranch on over 100 acres and built a log home near the historic buildings.

Born there in 1907, Dave had some wonderful tales of those early days, of playing around the old fort on the banks of the Fraser and how the sternwheelers would still stop, if needed, at the historic site. A man of great warmth and good humour, Dave's laugh rolled out repeatedly as he talked of a memorable trip on the old *BX*, called Queen of the North, when he was just a young lad. His mother took Dave, his sister, and a brother up to Fort George (today's Prince George) for a sports day one summer around 1915.

"Whenever you wanted the steamboat to stop, you just put out a white flag, then one of the big boats would put to shore near you," he recalled. "The *BX* stopped the most often. We had a little natural bay near the house; the crew would run out a plank, we would jump on and away we would go." The sternwheelers required little draught. The *BX* was just sixteen inches at the bow, twenty inches at the deepest point.

Going up to Fort George, the Twan family left at seven in the morning. The boat tied up at Cottonwood Canyon overnight, and they finally got to Fort George at one o'clock the next day. "We kids were all over the boat. We knew Captain Browne well and he even let us go up to his quarters at the very top." There was a special parlour in the stern for ladies, carpeted in red velvet, but it was the worst part of the boat in Dave's estimation, as it vibrated terribly from the paddlewheel.

"We even got down into the engine room, but we sure didn't hang around there," laughed Dave as he described the scene below decks where sweating men shoved wood by the cord into the big boilers. "Boy, was it ever hot!" Crews were stationed on shore all up and down the river, cutting great stacks of four-foot firewood to supply the boats. The deck hands required several hours to load it aboard and it was not unusual to see several rows of firewood piled high on the front lower deck.

Although the trip up to Fort George, bucking the current, was a long overnight one for the Twans, coming back was a different story. They left at seven in the morning and were home by noon. "I'll

*This 1981 photo of Dave was taken by the author and is set against the original Twan homestead and the remains of the Hudson's Bay Company's Fort Alexandria. (Photos courtesy John Roberts and* Williams Lake Tribune*)*

never forget coming down through those canyons," Dave said. "The captain had to get the boat going faster than the current to keep the boat under control. The whole nose would go under water and then come up again, spraying and flooding the lower decks. The doors and windows had to be locked tight so the water couldn't get in." Later he would remember that trip as one of the most exciting incidents in his life, one he wished he could have repeated.

Dave died in 1983, but he left a legacy of long ago Cariboo-Chilcotin stories to treasure.

*Fort Alexandria cairn on east side of Fraser River on Cariboo Highway. (Irene Stangoe photo)*

## Present of Salt
## Introduced her Parents

The young girl who had travelled all the way from Yale on a mule sat on a log beside Mud Lake and cried bitterly.

A tall good looking man strode over and asked her why she was crying. "I've no salt to put on my beans," she sobbed. The young man smiled and handed her a small package of the precious commodity from his vest pocket.

That little drama occurred one day in the early 1860s, at a place now known as McLeese Lake, and the couple who met at the camping spot on the way to the Barkerville gold fields were Alexander Douglas McInnes and Anna Elizabeth "Lizzie" Roddy. They later married and had five children. This story was told to me many years ago by their youngest daughter, Annie Huston of Soda Creek, who was born at Stanley in 1874.

Her father, who went by the name Douglas, was among the first group of miners to seek their fortune at Williams Creek. With his wife's assistance, he also ran a boarding house and they were there when fire swept through Barkerville in 1868, levelling most of it to the ground. Their son, Alex P. "Sandy" McInnes was just an infant at the time and his mother had to carry him up the hillside away from the creek to escape the heat and flames.

When the mines petered out in the early 1870s, McInnes moved his family to Fort Alexandria near Marguerite where he took up farm land and built a log stopping house, known as the 'McInnes House,' which served travellers on the Cariboo Wagon Road for many years. McInnes, a Glasgow Scot who ran his premises like an old country inn and kept the liquor under lock and key in a corner cupboard, also established a store and post office, and eventually became "mayor" of the little community.

*The McInnes House was a popular Cariboo inn for over fifty years, operated by Anne's parents and later her elder sister, Mary Rowed, pictured here in the 1930s. Attempts to preserve the buildings in the 1960s failed and nothing remains of the roadhouse. (BCARS E-05513)*

Lizzie McInnes was well liked by the natives who traded at the store, but not so Douglas. In fact, his stiff abrupt manner so offended a group of Chilcotins that they lay in wait to kill him one night on his customary rounds to lock up the chickens. But his wife fortunately took on the chore that night, and the natives fled.

This same straight-laced manner led his daughter, Annie, to elope with a stagecoach driver who made regular stops at their store on his way to and from Barkerville. Wayne Huston, who was born in Oregon, had been driving team since he was thirteen years old and was an expert horseman when he stepped off the train at Ashcroft. By the following day he was driving a BX stagecoach to Barkerville.

After their marriage, Annie moved from place to place up and down the Cariboo Road, making a home as close as possible to the 'section' he was driving. Thus their son Douglas was born at Quesnel, Claude at Ashcroft, and Inez at Lac la Hache.

In 1908 Wayne gave up the stagecoach trail, and for a few years ran the 59 Mile House before he finally settled his family at Soda Creek where he took over the store and post office. At that time Soda Creek was a bustling community where stages and teams met with the big river boats to carry freight and passengers farther up the river to Quesnel and Prince George.

*Drivers for Barnard's Express were known as temperate "land captains" and unparalleled horsemen who cared for their passengers and horses first and foremost and were respected by all. Here Wayne Huston readies his six-horse team near Ashcroft for another journey. Huston's pay cheque indicates that his pay was not issued until three weeks into August for July work! (Photo courtesy Ken Huston and Williams Lake Tribune)*

*In 1958, Annie Huston, then in her mid-80s was presented to Princess Margaret on her Royal Visit to the Cariboo (see Chapter 20).* (Williams Lake Tribune photo)

Tiny white-haired Annie Huston was in her 80s when I talked to her, but she could still remember two of the most famous sternwheelers—the *BX* and the *BC Express*—being built at Soda Creek. She recalled many trips on the big boats, and how one of the river boat captains liked to display his skill in navigation by trying to see how close he could come to a certain rock. Usually it was within two-and-a-half feet.

The coming of the PGE railway in 1919 spelled the beginning of the end for Soda Creek, but Wayne Huston, who died in 1942, did not see the final blow to the tiny village when the new highway completely bypassed it in 1954. His widow continued to live at Soda Creek in a little house beside the road her husband had travelled so often at the reins of a spirited team of horses. She died in 1963.

To finish off this saga of the McInnes family, I should mention that Sandy McInnes followed in his father's footsteps and was postmaster at Marguerite all his life. Before his death in 1946, he wrote down some of the fabulous stories he heard from his father and his good friend, Peter Dunlevy, who was credited with making the first major gold strike in the Cariboo on Horsefly River in June 1859, thus triggering the rush over the mountains to Antler and Williams Creek.

Published in book form by the Murray family at Lillooet, his memoirs are entitled simply *Dunlevey (sic)* and paint a vivid word picture of Jim Sellars, Tom Manifee, Tom Moffitt, and Ira Crow, the colourful, courageous men who accompanied Dunlevy in his quest for the elusive metal.

# Hog Tight and Bull Stout

As you drive into Williams Lake, one of the first names you see is "Boitanio." It is the name of the big mall to your right, the park nearby and, if you go further afield you will find the same name on a residential street. In the Springhouse area about twenty miles southwest of the city, there is also the pretty but shallow Boitanio Lake, originally called Salt Lake.

The name is one of the most historic in the Cariboo-Chilcotin and I personally will never forget Antone Boitanio. In my mind's eye, I can still see him, clad in black from his wide-brimmed hat down to his high-heeled cowboy boots, riding his big black horse in the Williams Lake Stampede parade, its silver gear sparkling in the sunshine. Always immaculately dressed, this white-haired gentleman with the flowing moustache seemed the epitome of an elegant Spanish don who had somehow strayed into the Cariboo.

He could trace his roots in the Cariboo back to gold rush days. His father, Augustine Boitanio, who was born in Favale, near Genoa, Italy in 1834, emigrated to the United States around 1857. The following year he struck out for British Columbia lured by stories of the gold to be found on the Fraser River.

There is no record of whether Augustine found any riches on the banks of the Fraser before he continued north. He probably followed the River Trail from Lillooet up through Dog Creek until he came to Alkali Lake. The rolling hills of forest and meadowland appealed to the young Italian and he set down roots, marrying Petqua, (later called Mary), a girl from the Alkali Lake Indian village. The couple had four children–Lawrence, Clotilda, Cecilia, and Antonio (known as Antone), who was born in 1885.

Instead of joining the gold-hungry men flocking to Barkerville, Augustine began packing to the mines, carrying as much as 200 pounds on his back. He then brought in jackasses for crossbreeding with local horses to sire mules which were marvellous pack animals, surpassing the average horse in endurance. According to Augustine's grandson, the late Buster Hamilton, it was the importation of these jackasses that led to the naming of Jackass Mountain, a familiar Fraser Canyon landmark.

One of the jackasses was unable to make the tremendous climb over the mountain on the trek north, he said, and had to be left there. When Augustine made his annual trip to the coast the following year, much to his surprise the jackass was still there–alive! On his return north, he picked up the animal and called the place "Jackass Mountain," as a reminder of the enduring little beast. Sounds reasonable . . . .

*This portrait of the founder of the Springhouse ranch, Agostino (Augustine) Boitanio was taken in Victoria by S.A. Spencer in 1877. (R. Armes Collection)*

As well as supplying mules for those in the transportation business, Augustine also had his own regular packtrains carrying supplies to the Interior for over thirty years.

Around 1884, Augustine decided to move his family and pre-empted land a bit further north on a high tableland now known as Springhouse. The area was originally called "St. Peter's Spring," a name which first occurs in Harry Guillod's *Journal of a Trip to Cariboo in 1862* in which he writes, "We camped at a place where there was a little spring and somebody had put up on a tree close by, 'St. Peter's Spring' with a cross executed in red chalk."

Augustine called his ranch "Springhouse" and I always presumed it was named for the spring some six or seven miles away mentioned by Guillod. But an article by historian Molly Forbes tells a different story–a story she was told by Clotilda, Augustine's daughter. After Augustine picked out his new homesite, she writes, he immediately dug a well and at thirty feet pure cold spring water gushed up "more precious to the pioneer settlers than the richest mine–and in gratitude he named his homestead 'Springhouse.' "

*This turn-of-the-century photo shows members of the small community that settled around Boitanio's Springhouse ranch. This home was destroyed by fire in the 1940s. (Photo courtesy T. Crosina)*

Augustine engaged in stock raising and ranching, with his two sons taking over in later years. Gradually a little settlement grew up around them, and when a post office was established at Springhouse in 1913, the first postmaster was Augustine Boitanio.

He was a tremendous worker. He built wagons of timber, the wheels thirty inches across and eight inches thick; his ranch was crisscrossed with split rail fences "hog tight and bull stout," and he made his own packsaddles, working and sewing the leather and canvas by hand. But there was time for a bit of fun too. After visiting there in 1901, Arthur Crease, the son of Judge Henry Crease, reported, "After supper they brought out the violins and we had a wonderful dance, quadrilles etc. I ordered a pair of gloves from Cecilia, a gifted glovemaker."

Augustine and his son Lawrence both died in 1914, so it was left to Antone to carry on with the ranch.

By this time Antone had married May Hamilton, daughter of the pioneer Hamiltons of 100 Mile House, and the couple had one daughter, Christine, who would later marry Ray Pigeon of Dog Creek (see story of the Pigeon family in *Cariboo-Chilcotin, Pioneer People & Places*).

Antone first worked as a packer along with his father, and as a cowboy for years. He had a keen eye for horse flesh, an attribute that no doubt contributed to his skill as a rider and also later as a judge of rodeo events. When Williams Lake came into being in 1919, Antone was there for the first stampede, riding in from Springhouse over the rough narrow trail to help stage what would later become Williams Lake's most

*May Boitanio poses in the 1930s. (Margaret Twan photo)*

important annual event and the second largest rodeo in Canada.

From then on Antone never missed a Stampede. Although he probably competed in some of the events at first, he was best known as a judge and could always be found in the judge's box, calmly and quietly deciding the merits of each ride. The big black horse and its rider dressed in black were an unforgettable part of each parade.

In 1942 Antone sold the Springhouse ranch and he and his wife moved into Williams Lake where they lived the rest of their lives. May died in 1958, but Antone was still here to lend colour and life to the Williams Lake Stampede for many more years. In 1958 he came out of retirement to make a rare appearance in the stampede arena to win the old timers' calf roping contest and the following month Princess Margaret presented the veteran contender with a prize of a trophy silver buckle and tooled belt. Antone continued to ride in the parade every year and won countless ribbons as best dressed cowboy right up until the time of his death in 1970 at 85 years.

When the Williams Lake Centennial Park Committee was looking for a name for the downtown park created in 1966 on the old golf course site, they chose "Boitanio" as they felt that Antone "typified the courage, colour and ingenuity of the men who settled the Cariboo." When a mall was built nearby in 1974, the owners too chose the pioneer's name.

*After making a rare arena appearance at the Williams Lake Stampede in 1957 and winning the old timers' calf roping contest at age 72, Antone Boitanio was presented with this belt and engraved buckle by Princess Margaret. (*Williams Lake Tribune *photo)*

In researching the Boitanios, there is little doubt that somehow over the years the name has been misspelled locally and should really be "Boitano" (without the extra "i") and pronounced "Boy-tan-o." This is the way it appears on early postal records and in correspondence.

A few years ago I had a visit from Louise Boitano of Puyallup, Washington, who has done extensive research on the name and even visited the picturesque mountain village of Favale in Italy where there are still many Boitanos.

"Most of the men are stonemasons and the homes are all built of stone with slate roofs," she said. Incidentally, the stone piers of the old Sheep Creek bridge over the Fraser River were built by Louis Boitano, Augustine's cousin, who came out from Italy for a visit sometime in the early 1900s. Although the bridge is gone, the piers can still be seen near the present Chilcotin bridge.

Louise has found Boitanos in Australia and throughout the United States, particularly in California where there is a Favalese Society. She also talked to Olympic figure skating champion Brian Boitano, and believes he is a descendant of the same family.

But no matter how it's spelled, there is no doubt that the Boitano name will not be forgotten in the Cariboo-Chilcotin.

# The Ranch Would Always Go Onward

I will never forget sitting in the living room of the Onward Ranch house, watching as the villain slithered down the dark staircase. Nearby the pure young maiden panted with apprehension and the upstanding hero stood staunchly prepared to do battle for his loved one.

The villain was my husband, and the historic Onward was the perfect setting for an old time melodrama staged by Williams Lake's internationally known playwright, the late Gwen Pharis Ringwood.

This happened sometime in the 1960s, but the story of the picturesque Onward Ranch, one of the oldest in the Cariboo and just eight miles south of Williams Lake, dates back to 1867 when Charles Boromeo Eagle, a Pennsylvanian of Dutch extraction, came north during gold rush days and acquired land along the pretty San Jose River.

His first home was a small log building, later used as a chicken house, but in 1886 he built a handsome new house, cutting the lumber on his own sawmill. He called his ranch "Onward" as he felt it would always progress and go onward.

A visitor that year, impressed with Eagle's ranch, described it in the Victoria *Daily Colonist*:

> The ranch lies beautifully and is well irrigated by a ditch seven miles in length, and carrying 1,000 inches of water from a permanent supply. Over 225,000 pounds of grain, 250,000 pounds of vegetables and 200 tons of hay are raised annually. Mr. Eagle has received numerous medals in Canada and Europe, and has now an exhibit of peas and potatoes at the Colonial exhibition.

A palatial residence, two-and-a-half storeys in height, was nearly completed at the time of our visit. It is probably the finest in the Interior, the superior decorating and finishing all done by hand. Black pine was used for the finer portions of woodwork and when polished and oiled makes an elegant finishing. The residence is supplied with many modern conveniences; its cost will be in the neighbourhood of $10,000.

Prior to this, Eagle had built a general store of hand-planed lumber and square nails for trading with natives and his numerous employees, as well as travellers going to and from the Chilcotin via the Chimney Creek valley.

Married to Annie Tatkwa, an Indian lady from the Bonaparte Reserve, Eagle had ten children, but four died at a tender age. In the cemetery at St. Joseph's Mission a few miles from the ranch are their four little graves, the smallest inscribed simply, "Lilia-age one hour." In a harsh land with no hospitals and doctors few and far between, it was not surprising that many children did not reach adulthood. Annie herself was only forty years of age when she died in 1897, just a few months after tiny Lilia. (Prior to her marriage to Eagle, Annie had lived common-law with John "Jock" Paxton Sr. and had one son, Tom.)

Probably the most intriguing story about the Eagle family, however, concerns their son, Charles W. "Willie" Eagle, who died a hero's death in South Africa following an attack by a lion.

Described as a well-read man with an excellent knowledge of tracking as well as being a top notch horseman, he joined the 5th Canadian Mounted Rifles at Kamloops and in 1899 went to fight in the second Anglo-Boer War. After peace was signed in 1902, he joined the South African police force, and was assigned to the Transvaal. According to the story reported in *Servamus*, the S.A. Police newsletter, he was patrolling on horseback near Messina on 24 September, 1908, when word reached him that two lion cubs had been killed and the lion and lioness were still in the vicinity.

As the lions were a danger to unsuspecting travellers, Eagle set out to find them. As he followed the tracks into a thicket, he was suddenly attacked by the enraged lions. He shot from the saddle and wounded them both, but the male sprang up and knocked Eagle to the ground, sinking its teeth into his right arm.

In an incredible feat of courage and desperation, Eagle managed to push the fingers of his left hand into the lion's nostrils and bend

*Charles B. Eagle migrated from Pennsylvania and built this majestic home in 1886 (the original log home is behind it). The store, which pre-dates the house, can be seen far right. The third owner, John Moore added the barn in 1911 (Photo courtesy John Roberts). The lower 1978 photo shows the home was further enhanced by Charles and Vivien Cowan during an extended ownership which started in 1920. (Williams Lake Tribune photo)*

its head backwards. Then, with lightning speed, he swung onto its back. Using his powerful legs, he kicked the lion so hard that it released his arm and then, weak from its wounds, it retreated into the woods.

Found by a Rhodesian engineer, Eagle was taken by wagon to Messina but there was no doctor available. Nine hours later he finally reached a hospital, but it was too late to save his life. He died October 10.

A memorial in his honour was erected by the Transvaal Police force near Fort Edward. The story of Eagle's heroism in *Servamus* ended with this tribute: "So died this Canadian in his new fatherland at the service of his fellow men and true to his calling as a policeman."

In the meantime, his brother Johnny, along with their half brother Tommy Paxton, had taken over the ranch following their father's death in 1890. Thus the firm of "Eagle and Paxton, Store Merchants" was born. The busy partners traded in everything–mustard plasters, steel spectacles, perfume, harmonicas, gunpowder, ladies blouses, painkillers, carriage bolts, and castor oil. Invoices reveal they paid $34.00 for two dozen moccasins, $4.32 for 24 pounds of jellybeans, and $15 for blacksmith bellows. But they soon became heavily indebted to the Harvey Bailey Co. of Ashcroft who supplied much of their stock, and when threatened with foreclosure, sold in 1903 to pioneer rancher John E. Moore for $9,500.

Ontario-born Moore had established a ranch at Alkali Lake around 1877, and married Annie Chiaro. The couple had six children, and years later their daughter Laura (Moxon) became a wonderful source of historical information for me.

One day in 1978 we went on a tour of her old home at the Onward, and she told me what it was like in 1903 when her dad took over the ranch. The store was empty except for some bolts of brightly coloured calico and odd sizes of boots, and the big house had no bathroom and no power, just coal oil lamps which had to be cleaned every day.

*The Onward was bought from the Eagle family by John Moore in 1903 and over the next seventeen years he restored its dignity and viability.*

*This early photo of Cowan, reputedly taken in London before the turn of the century, was used to promote Charles' big game hunting trips to the Yukon. (Photo courtesy Cowan's daughter Sonia Cornwall) Below, as a successful rancher in the 1930s.*

Her father restocked the store, refurbished the house, and built the Onward into a busy place again. Freight wagons and mule teams stopped there regularly, and dances held on the top floor of the warehouse attracted people for miles around. In 1911 he built a huge red barn near the house and store, which was not only utilitarian but a delight for photographers and artists alike.

"And up on the ridge behind the ranch," Laura recalled, "the Heyworth brothers—Leo, Gilson, and Gerald—had a mill and supplied the lumber for the very first buildings in Williams Lake." Around this time Moore decided to move into the new village and in 1920 sold the Onward to Charles G. Cowan and his wife Vivien of Kamloops.

Now I must digress a bit and tell you the fascinating story of Charles Cowan and how he convinced two English lords to invest in the Cariboo back in the early 1900s.

Born near Dublin in 1869, he was only fifteen when he followed an older brother to South Carolina. One day Charles happened to see a poster exhorting young men to join the North-West Mounted Police, and it sounded pretty thrilling to the young Irishman. Although a mite shy of the necessary six feet, he was accepted and stationed at Edmonton for the next six years.

The police experience then led him into big game hunting, guiding, and trapping. Some of his world record trophies ended up in New York's Rothschild Museum and the Kensington in London. Cowan, who was also known as "Dead-eye Dick" advertised in the London papers, and soon had a steady stream of British aristocracy booking for his trips to Alaska and the Yukon.

One was Lord Egerton of Tatton, and through him Charles met the Marquess of Exeter on one of his yearly trips to the old country. Well-liked among his English friends and often invited to their homes, Cowan soon convinced them to invest in Canada, or more specifically the Cariboo.

Thus the Marquess bought acres of land encompassing the 100 Mile House (Bridge Creek Estates) while Egerton acquired the 105, 108 and 111 Mile ranches, and both appointed Cowan to act as their agent to look after their holdings. (Lord Martin Cecil, the Marquess' son, came out in 1930 when just a lad of twenty-one, to take control of their 15,000 acre spread. Considered the "founding father" of the present 100 Mile town, he lived there until his death in 1988.)  By this time Cowan also owned two ranches in the Kamloops area, and maintained an office there, as well as acting as agent for the 134 Mile Ranch and the 150 Mile owned by the Cariboo Trading Co. When the Boer War broke out, he and his manager Evelyn Penrose tossed a coin to see who would go. Cowan lost (or did he win?) and journeyed back to the old country to form an Irish cavalry company, earning a medal in the conflict before returning to Kamloops.

When Cowan heard that Moore wanted to sell his Onward Ranch and had offered it to the government as the possible townsite for the "new" Williams Lake, he advised the Cariboo Trading Co. to grab it. "Otherwise I'll take it myself," he wrote.

The company didn't take up the option, so in 1920 for $20,000 the Cowans became the new owners of the Onward and immediately concentrated on "bringing back the land." Moore had devoted much of the valley to grain which had worn out the soil, so Charles Cowan sowed legume crops, then plowed them under and heavily fertilized the arid acres. He built miles of ditches and fencing, making his gates in the old store which he converted to a workshop. In 1929 the Cowans added the neighbouring historic 150 Mile Ranch to their holdings, but by this time Charles was in ill health and the family spent a great deal of time in Victoria, leaving John Zirnhelt to run the ranches. In 1939 when Charles suffered a massive stroke and died, Vivien returned to the Onward to become actively involved again.

A handsome gracious woman of tremendous creative ability, she also found time to pursue her talent for painting, and her home became the haunt of many artists, musicians, and creative people from all walks of life including A. Y. Jackson, one of the famous Group of Seven, who became her lifelong friend and frequent visitor to the Onward. He was here in 1945 when Vivien founded the Cariboo Art Society in her living room at the Onward, and agreed to be honourary life president.

After being acquired by the Cowans the Onward ranch house underwent many changes. Its stark lines were softened with a *porte-cochère*, a sun room, bay windows, and beautiful trees to shield it from the sun. Outside, the only tennis courts in the Cariboo drew tennis buffs from all over including the B.C. and Canadian champions, and the junior champion from Hungary, no less.

The Cowan's two daughters, Sonia and Druscilla, were both artistically inclined, with Sonia becoming well-known throughout Canada for her paintings of the Cariboo. She and her husband Hugh Cornwall, a grandson of Ashcroft pioneer Clement Cornwall, took over the management of the ranch in later years, and the lovely old-fashioned living room with its high ceilings continued to be the scene of many happy gatherings, musical evenings, bridge parties and of course the melodrama I remember so well.

In 1966 the Onward was sold again, this time to the Oblate Fathers from the nearby St. Joseph's Mission, but since 1980 has seen several changeovers. Both the Onward and Mission properties are now owned by the Cariboo Cattle Co. which plans to gradually restore the historic house to its former elegance over the next few years.

*After poor health claimed her husband, artist Vivian Cowan revitalized their Onward Ranch and founded the Cariboo Art Society. (Photo courtesy of daughter Dru Hodgson)*

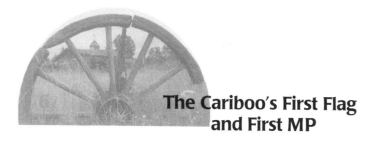

# The Cariboo's First Flag and First MP

*The origins of the first flag created in British Columbia are lost in time.*

*The flag, a beaver surrounded by a wreath of maple leaves on a white ground in the centre of the Union Jack, was flown in the Cariboo regularly until Confederation in 1871.*

*The man who is thought to have been a central figure in its creation was Joshua Spencer Thompson, editor and proprietor of the* Cariboo Sentinel, *published in Barkerville. Thompson practically ran the town and the district at the time of the gold rush.*

I found that item in a back issue of the *Tribune* one day, and was instantly intrigued by the description of our very first flag, and also the fact that Thompson was the Cariboo's first member of Parliament.

Born in Belfast in 1828 and a graduate of Trinity College at Dublin, Spencer emigrated to Canada from Northern Ireland in 1858 and settled first at Fort Hope (today's Hope).

Described as "a man of many parts with a varied experience and an aptitude for many things," he quickly settled into his new country and its politics. Incredibly, just two short years later, he was foreman of the Fort Hope Grand Jury, and as a representative of Fort Hope's interests, he condemned the absentee government of Governor James Douglas and demanded more responsible government, lower taxes and improved roads. At that time, Douglas was governor of both the Colony of Vancouver Island and the new colony of British Columbia on the mainland. His home was in Victoria, however, and he was often criticized for his lack of concern for the mainland.

*Joshua's flag? So rare that no genuine Cariboo flag has ever been re-
vealed. This design was illustrated in* Flags of the Old West *written by N.L.
"Bill" Barlee . Barlee wrote, "when the province finally joined Canada in
confederation, the unique flag from the Cariboo district was taken down
and never flown again. Sadly, no authenticated sample has survived." The
flag is reputed to have flown over Barkerville before 1871.*

In 1862 Thompson moved to Barkerville. I have no information
on why he left Fort Hope, but he was obviously a clever man who
saw the advantages of living in the booming new gold rush town. He
worked first as a clerk, then accountant, auctioneer, a mining commissioner, and later acquired interests in various mining claims. In
1866, he was elected to the Mining Board of the Cariboo, and by
1871 was foreman of the grand jury of Richfield. Not only that, but
he was the first chairman of the first school board to be formed in the
Cariboo. But Thompson didn't stop there. After acquiring the *Cariboo
Sentinel*, he became renowned for his speeches and editorials, and
was the Cariboo's most enthusiastic advocate of confederation.

So when was that first flag created? Well, in 1866 Vancouver
Island and the mainland became one territory under the name "Colony
of British Columbia" and it seems likely Thompson would suggest a
special flag be designed to mark the union of the two colonies. British
Columbia became Canada's sixth province on 20 July, 1871, and
Thompson organized an uproarious celebration in Barkerville on
the great day. An Order-in-Council declared that the "Cariboo
District" and the "Lillooet District" should constitute one district to
be designated "Cariboo District" and return one Member of
Parliament.

*Both before and after Confederation J.S.
Thompson served the Cariboo with distinction.
His deathbed wish suggests there was more to
Joshua than we will ever know. (BCARS
F-09728)*

Accordingly, on 20 December, 1871, a special election was held and Joshua Thompson was elected by acclamation as the first MP for Cariboo. He was reelected in 1872, 1874, and again in 1878. In the House of Commons, he called for improved postal and telegraphic com-munications, but above all he pushed for the completion of the Canadian Pacific Rail-way. Although elected as a "Liberal Conser-vative," he criticized both parties for delays in the railroad construction. According to the Victoria *Daily Colonist*, Thompson was always clear and effective in style, never descended into personalities and was never offensive.

Thompson was active socially in Barkerville too. Described as charming and hot-headed, he was a noted amateur singer and actor and became president of the Cariboo Literary Institute, manager of the Cariboo Amateur Dramatic Association, and helped establish the first library and first Freemason Grand Lodge in Cariboo.

Joshua Spencer Thompson died on 20 December, 1880 at Victoria. He had been in ill health for some time, but was determined to take his seat in the House. He managed to reach Victoria, but was

*This grand photo taken in Barkerville in the late 1860s includes Joshua Spencer Thompson, standing in the upper left window. Unfortunately we have been denied the top of the flagpole and a true glimpse of the elusive Cariboo flag. (BCARS A-03754)*

unable to carry on to Ottawa. Characteristically, it is said, this colourful figure met death while living in the best suite of the capital's best hotel, the Driard. He was just fifty-two.

Although he was extremely outgoing in nature, Thompson remained a mysterious figure. Accounts say that he never spoke of his past and was assumed to have been a bachelor. So it came as a surprise when he made a deathbed wish leaving his estate to a wife in San Francisco. The will was successfully contested by a relative.

Thompson, who was buried in the Ross Cemetery at the provincial capital, will always be remembered for his remarkable record of hard work and dedication to his adopted country, and particularly to the Cariboo which he represented so well.

# Pioneers of
## Chimney Creek Area

I wonder how many people today realize that when you drive out Highway 20 on your way to the Chilcotin, you pass through one of the most historic ranches in the Cariboo.

Known as the Chimney Creek ranch, or simply as Staffords, it is about ten miles south of Williams Lake and was pre-empted by pioneer Amedee Isnardy in the early 1860s. The two-storey home that he built over 100 years ago is still there, a lasting reminder of the young French adventurer.

Born in 1840 at Nice, France, Amedee was only fourteen years old when he and his two brothers stowed away on a boat heading for Mexico. From there the courageous teenager worked his way up into California and then into British Columbia around 1859.

Like many others, he was probably searching for gold as he drifted north. Following the Harrison route to Lillooet, he stayed there for a few years—operating a store and meeting Julienne Willamatkwa, believed to be the daughter of a Lillooet Indian chief.

By 1862 Amedee was on the move again and this time got as far as Chimney Creek where he was the first man to put down roots and settle in the valley—roots which now embrace one of the largest family trees in the Cariboo and include such names as Tresierra, Stafford, Grinder, English, Pinchbeck, Bowe, and more.

At that time, Chimney Creek was on one of the main routes into the Cariboo-Chilcotin, and Amedee was quite astute in establishing himself in the lush valley on a direct route to the gold fields. Called the Fraser River Trail, it was first trod smooth by native people, then the fur-traders, and finally eager prospectors who trekked up from Lillooet to Dog Creek, Alkali Lake and Chimney Creek, then on to

*This photo was taken after a nearby log saloon was added to Amedee Isnardy's original home at the turn of the century.*

Williams Lake and ultimately the fabulous diggings in the Cariboo Mountains.

Amedee and Julienne were married at St. Joseph's Mission, and lived at first in a small sod-roofed log cabin until they built the big roadhouse that still stands today. "I think it was built around the late 1860s or early 70s," says Mike Isnardy of Williams Lake, grandson of Amedee and Julienne. He was born in the frame house, as was his father Jimmy before him in 1879, so he knows it well.

"It was a big place with five bedrooms upstairs," he says, and was undoubtedly popular as a stopping house. The section made of hand-hewn squared timbers at the back was actually a saloon which was originally about a mile-and-a-half up the valley. "Cataline, the famous packer, often stopped there when he was going through on the Chimney Creek trail," says Mike. But around 1900 his grandfather, using teams of horses, moved the saloon down the valley and added it on to the stopping house.

"That's where freighters who had too much to drink stayed," says Mike, smiling. "It had three bedrooms upstairs, a small and large room downstairs." In later years, however, it was used for storing equipment, and finally in the 1970s was torn down.

When the Cariboo Wagon Road was built in 1862-5 and became the most popular route to the riches at Barkerville, the importance of Amedee's roadhouse must have waned. Although slight of build, Amedee was a wiry hard-working man and soon acquired more parcels of land. Eventually his huge ranch stretched all the way from the Fraser River up the Chimney Creek valley to Brunson Lake which was known as the "dairy ranch." This was originally pre-empted by a Charles Bronson (later spelled Brunson) who was a dairyman, stock raiser, and freighter.

The water rights for Chimney Creek registered in Amedee Isnardy's name in 1862 are believed to be the oldest in the Cariboo. To irrigate his farmlands, he hired fifty Chinese at fifty cents a day who, with pick and shovel, built a system of ditches along the valley. Even today some of the ditches can still be seen as they wind along parallel to the Chimney Lake road.

"Many of the Chinese were buried at the ranch," says Mike, "but in later years the bodies were dug up and shipped back to China."

As well as cattle, Amedee raised pigs and sheep and had a big vegetable garden. Although dates are a little sketchy, he also started operating a ferry (i.e. a small rowboat) across the Fraser, shuttling people and goods to and from the Chilcotin. Later he turned the operation of the ferry over to his eldest son, Joe, as evidenced by this 1891 news items from the *Victoria Colonist*: "Mr. J. Isnardy has put in tenders for the Chimney Creek ferry. He will run two boats:

*In 1904 the Chimney Creek or Sheep Creek bridge was completed revitalizing the entire area. It was destroyed in September 1962 after a new bridge was built. The original stone piers built by Louis Boitanio (see Chap. 4) are all that remains. (BCARS C-08790)*

one for passengers and the other for freight. Joe is an able young man and well fitted to pull an oar." This valuable service came to an end when the first bridge to be built across the Fraser at this point was opened in 1904.

Amedee and Julienne had eight children, but two died very young. Julienne was very devout and she would often travel by sleigh or wagon up the Chimney Creek trail to attend services at St. Joseph's Mission as there was no Williams Lake then.

Although the couple were quite strict, the Isnardy children grew up in a happy home full of music. While the bridge was being built between 1902-4, their big home was a busy place again with the bridge crews camping nearby, and joining the family for dances, parties, and races.

Amedee died in 1907, Julienne in 1918, and both are buried in the Mission cemetery. In his will, Amedee divided his land into five sections for his children—Frank getting pretty Brunson Lake ranch; Mathilda (Pinchbeck) the one at the Dog Creek road junction; Charlie the portion known today as Chimney Creek Estates; Hortense (Tresierra) Four Mile Creek ranch; Jimmy the Home ranch. Joe, the eldest, was left money.

*The youngest of six surviving children, Jimmy Isnardy continued to ranch the original family pre-emption for twenty years after his father's estate was settled. Jimmy was a talented musician, known throughout the Cariboo. (Photo courtesy Mike Isnardy)*

Jimmy, who in his early days packed with Cataline, was first married to Christine Bowe, then after her death to Evelyn Stafford. He continued to ranch the original land pre-empted by his parents until 1926 when he sold to John Moore of Alkali Lake and moved to Springhouse. After that it had a succession of owners until it was purchased by 1956 by Bill Stafford who still lives with his wife Beryl in the historic house.

The next time you drive out Highway 20 on your way to the Chilcotin, try to imagine it 130 years ago when it was a rough primitive trail travelled by freight wagons, mule-trains, and pioneers like Amedee Isnardy.

Another man who travelled this trail was Pablo Tresierra, a colourful pioneer freighter whose name is perpetuated in Pablo Creek and Pablo Mountain, and in his many descendants in the Cariboo-Chilcotin. He was described as slim, dark, and aristocratic-looking with a long moustache which he twirled up at the ends. He spoke English and Spanish fluently, but was a loner and often cantankerous.

About four miles or so after you've passed the old Chimney Creek ranch, you will see the entrance and sign for the Pablo Creek Ranch, often referred to as "Four Mile Creek." What you can't see from the highway is the cluster of historic buildings that mark the former home of Pablo and his wife Hortense.

The name "Tresierra" is Spanish and means "Three Mountains." Joseph Tresierra, the patriarch of the family, was born in Mexico in 1831, but it is believed his parents originally came from the Three Mountains area in Spain. During gold rush days, Joseph pushed north into California and finally ended up in British Columbia where he freighted by oxen from Yale to Barkerville.

On his way north, he met and married American-born Josephine. Their son, Pablo, was born at Yale in 1863 and he too became a freighter, driving bull wagons from Ashcroft to Becher's hotel and store at Riske Creek. Often they were loaded with whiskey.

It was probably on one of those trips that he met Hortense, the daughter of Amedee and Julienne Isnardy of the Chimney Creek Ranch. Following their marriage in 1886 at St. Joseph's Mission, the couple went to live on a chunk of land about four miles from Amedee's preemption. From then on it was known as the "Four Mile Creek Ranch" which is rather confusing as the stream itself is called "Pablo Creek."

The Four Mile CreekRanch developed by Pablo and Hortense became a handy stopping place for those travelling the River Trail north from Lillooet, winding up through Dog Creek, Alkali Lake and Springhouse. Even today the ruts of that old road can be still be seen meandering past the derelict buildings.

The couple had eight children. Hortense was a wonderful warmhearted lady with a heart of gold, and it was nothing to have forty or fifty friends and relatives gathering at the Tresierra home for a weekend.

*The Tresierras were an odd match; Pablo (r) was mostly an ornery loner while Hortense (l) had a heart the size of their ranch. Even in 1995 the small home and outbuildings retained their rustic majesty. (Photo courtesy Alice Tresierra and* Williams Lake Tribune)

But eventually Pablo and Hortense decided to go their separate ways, with Hortense moving to the Peavine Springs ranch near the Fraser River bridge with her second husband Frank English. In later years she was fondly known as "Peavine Granny."

Pablo continued to live and work in the Cariboo, mostly in the Big Bar area. He died at Williams Lake in 1941, and Hortense in 1956. At the time of her death it was reported that she was survived by 55 grandchildren, 101 great grandchildren, and seven great great grandchildren which gives you some idea of the size of this old Cariboo family.

After the Tresierras left Four Mile Creek Ranch, it had a succession of owners. A partnership of Dr. C. A. Boyd of 150 Mile and R. N. Barrowman owned it for twenty years. A 1912 report says, "In extent it is about 1000 acres with 175 acres under crops which include tomatoes, pumpkins and citrons which find a ready market."

In 1933 it was acquired by Donald and Bella Mackay. Beef drives were a common sight on the Chilcotin road by then, and Four Mile Creek Ranch became a popular stopover before the final push to the stockyards at Williams Lake. The Mackays also raised sheep which did well on the side hills of the Fraser. In later years Bella would recall roasting a whole lamb and baking eight pies at a time, which with the onslaught of hungry cowboys, would disappear in one meal.

They sold in 1948 to a Victoria man, then it reverted back to the original family again when Mike Isnardy and his brother Amedee (named for his grandfather) took it over. In the late 1960s it was purchased by Karl and Reta Seibert, the present owners, who changed the name to "Pablo Creek Ranch." and registered their own "PC" brand. "We are still using the barn and sheds for storage," says Reta, "but the rest of the old buildings are gradually disintegrating."

Soon another little bit of Cariboo-Chilcotin history will be gone.

# Barkerville Tales

## A Gold Rush Tragedy

The sad story of John A. "Cariboo" Cameron who made a fortune at Barkerville in gold rush days, but led a tragic life thereafter is a classic Cariboo tale which has been told many times. Various accounts differ in some details, but this one is based on the story as related by local historian Alf Baynes.

Cameron and his wife Sophia, along with their year-old daughter, left their home at Glengarry near Cornwall, Ontario, early in 1862 to journey to B.C., hoping to strike it rich in the Cariboo mountains. Arriving at Victoria, the first tragedy struck the family when the little girl, weakened by the long trip through the Panama Canal, became ill and died just five days later.

During this time, the grief-stricken couple became friends with Robert Stevenson, a storekeeper at Antler Creek visiting Victoria. When he offered the Camerons a partnership in the store, the couple accepted and arrived in the Barkerville area in July with a shipment of stock which included such necessities as candles, nails, and butter, which all sold for $5 a pound, and matches at $1.50 a box. But like so many others, the two men were principally interested in gold and began staking and working claims.

Sophia was a tall beautiful girl, just 28 years of age, and one of the few women in Barkerville at that time. One can only imagine the incredible hardships she must have endured in the raw primitive mining camp. In September Sophia became very ill with typhoid, or mountain fever as it was called, and died October 23 despite the

*One of Barkerville's most tragic love stories befell John Cameron, the man who made the Cariboo gold rush's richest strike. Margaret Sophia (nee Groves) Cameron's marriage and days as the beauty of Barkerville were short-lived. (BCARS A-01155 and D-07952)*

efforts of local doctors. Her deathbed request was to be buried in Ontario if John "struck it rich."

It was a bitterly cold day with the thermometer registering minus 30 degrees on the morning she died. Cameron arranged for his wife's body to be enclosed in a double tin and wooden coffin, and placed in an empty cabin following the simple funeral.

In December John and his partner did indeed strike it rich, taking out an estimated $800,000 in gold ($6 million at current values). In January he and his partner Stevenson enlisted twenty-two miners to help take Sophia to Victoria. He could well afford to pay them $12 a day plus a bonus if they stuck with him. And so began the weirdest funeral cortège in history. Sophia's body was lashed to a toboggan along with food, blankets, and gold, and the horrendous trip began, over the mountains and through deep snow in minus 50 degree weather. In the first eleven days they covered only seventy-two miles.

At Beaver Lake they noted ninety snow graves (temporary resting places until the frost came out of the ground) containing the bodies of native people who had died in the smallpox plague that winter, while further on at Williams Lake they recorded 125 snow graves.

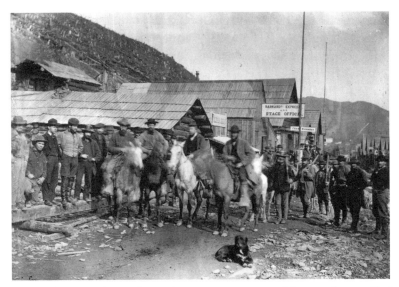

*This 1863 crew of armed guards were a separate gold escort but typified the band of local miners Cameron hired to join his procession to the coast. (BCARS A-03148)*

From there on the going was easier so many of the miners returned to Barkerville. Cameron and Stevenson carried on, taking the Lillooet-Douglas route to the coast (the Cariboo Wagon Road was not completed yet), and finally arrived in Victoria on March 6, thirty-six days after their departure from Barkerville. A special coffin filled with alcohol was made for Sophia, and a second funeral attended by 800 former and would-be miners was held.

Cameron then returned to Richfield to work on his claim, which turned out to be rich beyond his wildest dreams. The town which sprang up around his diggings became known as Camerontown.

In October he was back in Victoria to carry out his mission to take his wife's body back to Glengarry. The coffin was shipped via the Panama Canal to Ontario. There, before the third funeral was held in Cornwall, Mrs. Cameron's father asked to see his daughter's face one more time. But Cameron refused, and no persuasion could move him.

Soon rumours abounded that the coffin contained not Sophia's body, but that of a native woman. In another version, it was alleged that Cameron had sold his wife to an Indian chief and concocted the story of her death. Cameron refused to open the casket for nine years, but finally agreed. When the body was exhumed, the late Mrs.

Cameron was identified by her father and the rumours—and Sophia—were finally laid to rest once and for all.

By this time John Cameron had remarried. He built a lavish mansion, and over the years due to poor investments and extravagant gifts to family and friends, managed to lose his fortune.

Impoverished by 1886, Cameron returned to British Columbia with his wife Emma, where he worked in the Big Bend mines for a time. Then in September, 1888, he returned to Barkerville. But he was too late; the gold was gone and he died there two months later of a massive stroke, a broken and penniless man of 68. He is buried in the historic cemetery there.

## Josephine, The Dance Hall Queen

This leads me to a story I found in a 1951 issue of *The Williams Lake Tribune*–one that is strangely similar to Cameron's.

It concerns Josephine, a dance hall queen who also died at Barkerville in gold rush days sometime in the 1860s.

According to the story, Josephine too made a deathwish and asked to be buried in San Francisco. One of her miner friends then volunteered to make the long journey in the middle of winter to Yale where a tinsmith was engaged to return with him and make a coffin.

In the meantime the dance hall queen occupied a temporary grave in a snowmound guarded from molestation by wolves and dogs by a four-man guard who were on duty twenty-four hours a day.

When the Yale tinsmith had completed the coffin, a quantity of tin was left over and this was expertly fashioned into two dozen beer jugs and sold to the saloon keeper.

Eight miners carried Josephine in her coffin to Yale from where the body was shipped to San Francisco for burial.

The entire funeral was reported to have cost $30,000, a fortune in those days, but the miners were happy and satisfied. Like Robert Service, they were faithful believers in the axiom that "a promise made is a debt unpaid."

This story was related to the Prince George Rotary Club in December 1951 by Constance Cox whose uncle had been one of the first miners to discover gold at Barkerville.

She had amassed many historical artifacts over the years, and included in her collection was one of the beer jugs made from the tin left over from Josephine's coffin.

*Is Josephine here? We'll never know but these anonymous "hurdy-gurdy" girls of 1865 were treated as ladies and earned their employer one dollar per minute for sharing a dance. (BCARS G-00817)*

## Friends Forever

The late Bob Campbell of Horsefly was a great historian and writer, and occasionally I come across his stories, heart-warming little vignettes not to be found in ordinary historical books.

I found this one in Quesnel's *Cariboo Observer* dated June 25, 1927, and it concerns two miners who came from the south of England together to join in the rush to the Cariboo gold fields in the 1860s. Their names were Cyr Roe and Frank Orr.

Although written in the flowery language of an earlier age, I find it a fascinating tale of early Cariboo days. Campbell writes:

> One reads occasionally of strong attachments between individuals, but the friendship and loyalty of these two sterling, sturdy prospectors had few parallels, even in fiction. Cy was

tall, gaunt, expressionless though kindly; Frank was broad, smiling and cheery.

From boyhood to old age, these two kindred spirits held an abiding faith and affection for each other, rare among mortals, which endured until they were laid away side-by-side in the Barkerville cemetery.

The men were expert miners and consistent prospectors. During their 30 years of activity in the Cariboo, they were never separated for a single day, or ever known to have any differences.

Whether at work in their tunnels or celebrating amongst a merry crew, they were nature's noblemen, kindly and great hearted, and highly respected by all who knew them intimately. Like most prospectors when fortune favoured them, they were generous to a fault. Their door was always open, and a hearty welcome was extended to their kind.

Suddenly in the late 90s, Cy became seriously ill, Frank nursing him with the tenderness of a brother. Despite heroic efforts, Cy became worse and was moved to the Barkerville hospital where a short time later he died with his hand tenderly clasped by his faithful partner.

Then a strange thing happened. Frank showed no open sign of grief over his great loss, though the ever present smile on his open countenance had disappeared. Instead a strange calm possessed him. He quietly arranged for his partner's funeral, and settled up their partnership affairs.

He stood stolidly and bareheaded beside the postmaster, James Stone, who read the burial service, and watched with steadfast eye until the last shovelful of mould rounded up Cy's last resting place. He then turned and walked quietly and deliberately to his lonely miner's cabin.

Next morning a neighbour opened the door of the humble dwelling. Frank lay quietly as if asleep on his bed. On the table beside him lay a sheet of notepaper, and on it was scrawled these terse lines: "I am gone to meet Cy. Frank."

Close by on the table was a glass containing the dregs of potassium cyanide.

# The First Williams Lake and the Hanging Judge

Many of you have heard of the Sir Matthew Baillie Begbie, the famous "hanging judge" of Cariboo gold rush history, but did you know he often dispensed justice at Williams Lake?

An imposing man, over six feet tall, with piercing eyes, a Van Dyke beard and carefully waxed moustache, Begbie was a familiar figure in his black lawyer's clothes as he travelled on foot or horseback throughout the Cariboo. He always wore his official robes when he held court whether it was in a saloon, tent, stable or a rough log courthouse like the one at the first Williams Lake settlement, later known as the Comer, about three miles northwest of the present downtown core.

It was here that he presided over the trial of Gilchrist, an American who pulled a gun during an argument while gambling in a local saloon, and in the resulting fracas, killed a man sitting at the bar. When the jury returned a verdict of manslaughter, Begbie angrily rose to his full height and thundered, "Prisoner, your crime was unmitigated, diabolical murder. You deserve to be hanged. Had the jury performed their duty, I might now have the painful satisfaction of condemning you to death."

Turning to the jury, he said, "And you, gentlemen, are a pack of Dallas horse thieves and permit me to say that it would give me great pleasure to see you hanged, each and every one of you, for declaring a murderer guilty of manslaughter."

From cases like this, repeated over the years, the legend grew that Begbie was a "hanging judge." He did hand down the death sentence on occasion, but only after a jury had found the prisoner guilty of murder. He never took part in any executions. There were

*Judge Matthew Begbie's harsh words and stiff penalties have become synonymous with Cariboo justice and some of his hanging edicts were dispensed in Williams Lake.(BCARS 24288)*

many recorded trials which helped build Begbie's reputation for being stern and ruthless in maintaining British law and order and controlling the violence that could have erupted in those frantic gold rush years.

Another famous incident at Williams Lake happened in 1863 when he sentenced four natives to death for the murder of two Italians at Springhouse. Lazaro Monteverde and a companion were slogging up the Fraser River Trail in early July, heading for Amedee Isnardy's stopping house at Chimney Creek, when they were jumped by mounted natives, shot and dragged off the trail.

The natives apparently believed the Italians were carrying gold but all they got was a measly $67, according to Begbie's notes of the trial. On the stand, one of them confessed that, "there were no angry words except the Italians ordered them (us) off the trail. I was rather drunk . . ." An unverified story says the Indians did indeed obtain gold and jewelry from the two victims and buried it somewhere. If so, it has never been found.

The trial in October lasted one day and Begbie's notes end with this terse comment: "Verdict: guilty against all four. Sentence: death." Two were only sixteen years old. One man escaped custody, but was captured two years later and executed at New Westminster. The other three were hanged 4 December, 1863, at Williams Lake and buried near the jail.

Years later, in an article written for the 1926 Stampede booklet, Cariboo historian Louis Le Bourdais described the scene of the hanging: "Standing alongside the old log jail, its perfect dovetailed corners bearing mute evidence of truly remarkable workmanship at the 'upper place,' visualize the scaffold just behind it, the three condemned men, handcuffed and blindfolded, each escorted by a policeman, and the great concourse of Indians convoked for the purpose of listening to a 'moral lecture with illustrations.' "

This took place at what I like to refer to as the "first Williams Lake," now known as the Comer area. When I look at the bare unattractive hillside crisscrossed with rough dirt roads up behind the present Weldwood mill, I find it hard to imagine that it was once the site of a thriving community.

As well as the jail, there was a government building, two roadhouses, as well as several homes, numerous barns and stables, and an old Indian church and settlement. It was headquarters for the gold commissioner, and postal centre for the Cariboo.

All vestiges have now completely disappeared, but during gold rush days it was one of the most important settlements in the Cariboo until bypassed by the Cariboo Wagon Road in 1863. (See *Cariboo-Chilcotin, Pioneer People & Places*). Pioneers William Pinchbeck and William Lyne stayed and eventually owned the entire valley, with the first Williams Lake settlement becoming the headquarters of their vast farming enterprise. A big stopping house dominated the valley. Although it has been difficult to establish its exact history, a large frame roadhouse was apparently added onto one of the original log structures, (perhaps the courthouse/government building). This could have been sometime in the late 1860s, or perhaps early 1870s.

With its eight bedrooms, bar, store, and restaurant, it was a busy place. Miners came and went, stayed for the winter, and frequented the bar where Pinchbeck served his famous White Wheat Whiskey at two-bits a shot. And of course Begbie stayed there on his circuits through the Cariboo.

After Pinchbeck built a handsome new home down by the lake for his English bride in 1884, his first roadhouse became known as the "Upper House" and was still maintained as an integral part of his big ranch. Following his death in 1893, the ranch was leased for some years, then purchased in 1899 by Robert Borland, owner of the 150 Mile Ranch, for $17,000. He lived in the new "Lower House" by the lake with his young bride, but sold or leased the upper part to Mike Minton who some years earlier had pre-empted land and founded the Chilco Ranch on the south side of the Chilcotin River near Hanceville.

Described as a big humorous Irishman, Minton will always be

*After Uncle Mike's death Mamie Comer, pictured here, and her two brothers managed the property. One simple improvement made at Comer House (see earlier photo on right) was to remove a strip of railing and allow direct access to their front door.*

remembered by the creek on the Chilco which bears his name.

When Minton took over at Williams Lake his two orphaned nephews, Bill and Tommy Comer came from their home in Minneapolis to help run the ranch while he tried his luck in the great Yukon gold rush. The nephews brought with them their beautiful sister, Mamie.

When Minton died in 1904, the two brothers continued to operate the ranch and thus the old stopping place became known as the Comer House, and the surrounding meadows as the Comer Ranch.

I don't have much information on the Comers except that Bill died at an early age, and Mamie married and moved to California. Tommy stayed in the Williams Lake area where for twenty-five years he was the government road foreman for the Cariboo-Chilcotin region. In fact Tommy was the muleskinner when the first snowplow to be seen in the new village of Williams Lake was brought up from

*The Upper House was built at the original settlement of Williams Lake and pre-dated the famous Cariboo Wagon Road which bypassed this site. This wonderful photo, complete with one of the Cariboo's oldest Russell fences shows the grand frame home built by the two pioneer Williams (Pinchbeck and Lyne) who farmed the entire valley. (Photo courtesy Rhona Armes).*

*The relentlessness of time was unkind to Upper House later known as the Comer House. In the late 1800s William Pinchbeck's wife and sister pose to the right of Mr. and Mrs. Lyne. Begbie's guest room was on the far right of the second floor. By the 1920s the deterioration was obvious and most of it was razed in 1925, leaving the solid log portion. (extreme left of inset photo)*

the Public Works headquarters at 150 Mile House in 1923. A huge affair made of two-inch planks, it was pulled by a team of sixteen horses. Tommy died in 1949 and is buried in the Williams Lake Cemetery.

The Comer property, which covered 1,000 acres, was sold around 1913, along with the rest of the original Pinchbeck/Borland ranch, to the Pacific Great Eastern railway which was being pushed up through the interior of the province. It finally reached the Williams Lake area in 1919, and when the streets of the new village were laid out, one was named "Comer" for the three young people who had carved a niche for themselves in the annals of Williams Lake history.

By 1919 the frame part of the Comer House was disintegrating. Harry Curtis, who established the first sawmill at Williams Lake in 1919, lived there with his family for a short time. His son, Colin Curtis, remembers the place was deserted and the windows broken. "We had to put up canvas to keep the flies and mosquitoes out." Percy Clarke, his wife and son Ben also lived in it for a few years, and Ben later remembered there was an old sign in the yard pointing towards Soda Creek which read "Barkerville Trail." Traces of the historic route were still discernible.

In 1925 the dilapidated frame addition of the Comer house was torn down, leaving the sturdy two-storey log section still intact. I believe this was where Pinchbeck had his popular bar in earlier years, and it became home for Richard Kinvig and his family from 1926 to 1936.

*This log structure, thought to be the original courthouse, then part of the Pinchbeck roadhouse and saloon, was home to Richard and Mrs. Kinvig and was still a sturdy abode in the middle of the Depression, known as the Comer House. (Photo courtesy Winnie Gavelin)*

*Mrs. P.P. Clarke, property resident in the early 1920s, stands with her sister in front of the original jail where prisoners had awaited Judge Begbie's wrath six decades earlier. The front was cut out in later years so it could be used as an implement shed. (Photo courtesy Winnie Gavelin)*

His daughter, Winnie Gavelin of Lower Nicola, remembers those years well. As well as the house and old jail, there was still a large barn, machine shed, chicken house, and another small two-room house. "My dad worked up the fields and grew good crops of wheat and oats, and cut it with a binder which was pulled by three horses. He also had a large garden and sold the vegetables to the stores in Williams Lake."

"We had twelve cows which were milked by hand . . . the cream was sent by PGE railway to the Quesnel creamery in five-gallon cans. Mr. and Mrs. Edwards also had a dairy on property below the Comer along the PGE tracks. They called it the Glendale Dairy."

In 1947 when Edna and Lionel Singlehurst moved onto the Comer and established their Primrose Dairy, some of the old buildings were still there although the massive logs were clearly collapsing. The old jail, which had been converted to an implement shed in later years, was demolished and burned sometime in the 1950s. It was the last of the original structures to go.

The last person to lease the old Comer site was Adolf Beyerle, and by that time (1960) there were only a few rotting logs lying on the ground, all that remained of the first Williams Lake settlement.

A few years ago local historian Dave Falconer erected a large wooden cross high on the hillside overlooking the historic site. It is inscribed "Here lie three Indians, hanged near here by Judge Begbie, 1863." A bit macabre perhaps, but it is the only link to Williams Lake's colourful past which included the famous "Hanging Judge."

# A New Site
# and a New Future

Another bit of Cariboo-Chilcotin history was preserved twenty years ago when two old buildings at Hanceville were moved to a new site and a new future.

Soft-spoken Bob Shaw, a mechanic by trade, loves to collect and restore antique machinery and in 1977 was looking for some salvageable logs to make into an old-style blacksmith shop on his property at Chimney Valley Estates, about ten miles southwest of Williams Lake.

A friend happened to mention that the original stores at Lee's Corner in the Chilcotin were earmarked for destruction with the re-building of Highway 20; in fact, one had a survey ribbon dead centre in the middle of it.

After looking them over, Bob decided to buy the smaller one which had been built in the 1880s by Finlander Dan "Ole" Nordberg who operated it as a trading post for a number of years, selling out in 1891 to rancher Norman Lee.

Bob also inherited an intriguing story when he purchased the small log building. Apparently Nordberg did not trust banks and "squirrelled away" ten and twenty-dollar gold pieces in all kinds of nooks and crannies. After Lee bought the store it was said that he kept digging the coins out of the "flour bin, the tea chest, the rice barrel, and other odd places."

Bob admits with a smile that he lifted the floor very carefully when it came time to move the old trading post "just in case something had gone through." But even though he used a metal detector, he didn't find a thing. Others appeared to have been before him as

*Above, Bob Shaw surveys his 1977 purchase, the original Nordberg Trading Post at Hanceville. Once hooked on restoration, he is shown on the roof of a second store, turning it into his family home. This structure was built in 1925 by Norman Lee. (*Williams Lake Tribune *photos)*

*Norman Lee's Hanceville store is one of a number of Cariboo-Chicotin structures that have been preserved by a widespread community proud of its heritage.*

the dirt looked as though it had already been dug up and sifted very carefully.

The second owner of the little store was a man who became a legendary figure in his own time. Norman Lee emigrated from England in 1882 and a few years later went into partnership with Hugh Bayliff, another Cariboo pioneer who founded the Chilancoh Ranch near Redstone.

But in 1891 Lee struck out on his own, bought the Nordberg store and cabin, and established his own Beaver Ranch at what became known as Lee's Corner at Hanceville. Times were tough, and when the struggling rancher heard of the great Klondike gold discoveries in 1897, he decided to drive 200 head of beef cattle north over 1500 miles of rugged country to the meat-hungry miners.

His diary of the incredible but ill-fated venture in which he lost all his cattle and ended up simply with a dog, a dollar, and a blanket, is chronicled in *Klondike Cattle Drive* (Heritage House).

Despite this disaster, Lee returned to carry on with his ranch and the trading post started by Ole Nordberg. Years later, in 1925, he had the Scallon brothers of Big Creek build him a larger store which his wife, Agnes, known throughout the Chilcotin as "Gan-Gan," would operate for many years.

This remarkable English-born lady came to Canada as a bride in 1903, arriving at the CPR depot in Ashcroft on February 10 in 50-below weather. The couple then traveled by horse-drawn sleigh

*Agnes Lee was affectionately known as "Gan-Gan." She continued to operate her store for almost twenty years after her husband's death, until she was eighty-six.*

to their rough log home in the wilderness at Hanceville, a 200-mile trip which took seven long bone-chilling days.

Agnes was terribly homesick at first, but then settled down and came to love her new country. She had a special place in her heart for Indian people and mastered the difficult Chilcotin language so she could more easily converse and trade with native people who frequented her store.

Norman died in 1939 and son Dan carried on with the ranch while his mother continued to run the store, despite failing eyesight, until 1957. That's when her historic log store, with its bolts of bright cotton prints, bins of household staples, and lanterns and harness hanging from the rafters, closed forever. A new Lee's Corner Store and Cafe was built nearby that same year.

Agnes died a year later at 87 years of age, just a few months after being presented to Princess Margaret (see chapter 20).

After 1957 both Nordberg's original trading post and Gan-Gan's store were used for implement and storage sheds for some years until they were scheduled for demolition in the upgrading of the Chilcotin highway in the 70s.

Then Bob Shaw bought the Nordberg store which he took down log by log. Marked with metal tags, the logs were then trucked to and reassembled on his property overlooking Chimney Creek. The huge 22" diameter logs had been hand-hewn with broad axes and held together with square nails, a process entirely different from contemporary log construction. From the first Bob was fascinated with the old time carpentry work—then he was hooked.

Originally he had planned to build a modern home of new logs alongside his rebuilt pioneer store but reclaiming Nordberg's little outlet changed his mind—especially after he heard the second store had still not been demolished. This time he had to get a crane out to Lee's Corner to lift the roof off in sections as he did not want to drop it on the hand-hewn beams. Then like the first store, the logs were marked, taken down one-by-one, and trucked to its Chimney Creek site, some seventy-five miles away.

Bob Shaw's troubles were not over. Some of the old logs were twisted, which made reconstruction difficult. He also had to cut the height down by two rounds, then manipulate those logs to fill in the end where the entrance to the store had been. "It was a long way up there," he said, as he described the height of the original 27x44-foot building. "It's amazing what they did with horses and hand tools back then."

He also had the old logs sandblasted to remove the weathering and dirt accumulations of over fifty years, and restore them to a golden sheen. "It hasn't been cheap," he observed. "I could have bought peeled logs and built a new home with what it cost to bring the old buildings over and rebuild them."

Today Bob and his wife Glenna live comfortably in their old-new home surrounded by the beauty of logs expertly cut and hewn many years ago. "I'm quite happy; it has worked well," he says. He also has a roomy workshop in the old trading post for his blacksmithing hobby doing creative metal and mechanical work on his anvil and forge, "things that make big noises and bad smells."

Among the treasures he is restoring are the old steam engines from the Graham, Knoll and Bell ranches in the Chilcotin, which also reflect a way of life that has gone forever.

# Captain Watson's
# House of Mystery

I first saw the Watson Mansion on Tatton Road near the 108 Mile House in 1974, and can remember being absolutely appalled at the wanton destruction of what had once been a magnificent home. The house had been completely vandalized; the doors gone and windows smashed. The heavily embossed wallpaper hung in shreds, wood panelling had been torn from the walls, and even the fireplaces of costly Italian marble had been demolished.

As I picked my way through the debris littering the floors, I tried to imagine what it must have been like in its heyday when stagecoaches and freight teams lumbered up the Cariboo Wagon Road and a handsome young officer waited in vain for his ladylove.

The story behind the historic mansion, which was sometimes referred to as the "House of Mystery," is touched with sadness, although there doesn't seem to have been a single ghost or unsolved crime lurking in its past.

Captain Geoffrey Launcelot Watson, a former British army officer with the York and Lancashire Regiment, was six-and-a-half feet tall, a superb horseman and a crack shot. Educated at Eton, he joined up when he was just twenty to go and fight in the Boer War. When or why he came to Canada seems to be a bit of a mystery, but he arrived in the Cariboo in the early 1900s and immediately fell in love with the rolling countryside. A man of some wealth, Watson acquired 50,000 acres north of 100 Mile House, some under government grant, some for $25 per acre. His purchase included the 108 Mile property pre-empted in 1863 by William Roper, later owned by famed BX stagecoach driver Steve Tingley.

*The historic 108 Mile Ranch evoked the essence of Cariboo life for decades. This photo, taken in the late 1800s, preceded the construction of Capt. Watson's famed Clydesdale barn, one of the largest log barns in Canada. (BCARS D-08070)*

Watson then commissioned a Victoria architect to design a gracious country home to which he hoped to bring his English bride-to-be. He began construction in 1904, using mostly local timber, but also hauling special materials and rich furnishings by eighteen-horse freight wagons from the railhead at Ashcroft.

Three storeys high, it was indeed a gorgeous house. Each room was beautifully appointed, many filled with the delicate ivory artifacts and other luxury items the captain had gathered from around the world.

Capt. Watson's ranch, with its slaughterhouse, bunkhouses, icehouse, and store, was a beehive of activity during the years he lived in the Cariboo. With breeding stock imported from Scotland, he reputedly built up a herd of 10,000 Highland cattle, and in 1908 constructed a huge log barn especially for his 100 purebred Clydesdale horses. Appropriately enough, he named it "Highland Ranch" to reflect his proud Scottish ancestry.

But the English girl who was to be the chatelaine of this rangeland manor, built several miles from the main ranch buildings, never saw the lovely home designed especially for her. When she heard that two renegade natives, wanted for murder, were roaming the countryside, she decided that life in the wild and remote Cariboo was not for her. Some say the house was promptly dubbed "Watson's Folly" but despite his disappointment Capt. Watson continued to live and work on his beloved Cariboo ranch.

The late Gilbert Forbes of Lac la Hache who was manager of the 105 Mile ranch around this time, remembered the Captain well.

"He used to have a big elephant gun which I think he kept just for the pleasure of seeing it (the recoil) knock us down," he wrote in his memoirs. "He also had a team of reindeer and in winter would take all the kids for rides." Forbes recalled that remittance men from England called "mudpups" stayed at the ranch. He believed "Cap," as he called him, was a rich man on account of Watson's Scotch whiskey, a family enterprise.

A lover of fine horseflesh, the captain was also the proud owner of two pairs of sulky horses which were said to be the most beautiful animals for miles around. And for a change of pace, he loved to get behind the wheel of his prized Cadillac car. Described as an extremely kind and generous man, the captain was idolized by the native people whom he frequently helped out if they were in need; giving them a horse, feeding an entire family and of course hiring them for ranch work. Most were superb horsemen who were invaluable on the frequent cattle drives to the railhead at Ashcroft.

*Here, a sign of the Circle S Ranch is propped against the verandah of the Watson mansion after restoration. (Don Robertson photo)*

In 1915 after the outbreak of World War I, the captain was called up and returned to England, and in 1917 was killed in action in France. The property was eventually acquired by Lord Egerton of Tatton, England, who appointed Charles G. Cowan of the Onward Ranch near Williams Lake (see Chapter 5) to act as his agent. Cowan sometimes stayed a month or so at the Watson Mansion during hunting season, but other than that, it remained empty, gradually disintegrating over the years as time and vandals took their toll.

After my initial trip in 1974 to see the abandoned house, which by that time had become part of Henry Block's 108 Recreational Ranch, I returned again in 1980 after hearing reports of the mansion's rejuvenation.

Dozens of youngsters ringed the corral fence, and inside a young chap was playing a lively tune on an electronic organ in the parlour-foyer where Capt. Watson probably paused to warm himself by the grand fireplace after a day's hunting.

The smell of frying chicken wafted in from the big old fashioned kitchen. On the second floor, the six bedrooms which once held canopied four poster beds were now crammed with rustic bunk beds.

Thanks to Henry Block who had donated 90 acres of land for the cause, it was now the headquarters for a youth camp called Circle Square Ranch where youngsters could learn to ride and enjoy a western atmosphere. Massive amounts of money had been spent on transforming the decaying mansion into a solid comfortable building again, although it naturally was not as elegant as it had been in Capt. Watson's day.

Sadly, this new lease on life did not last long. On Christmas Eve, 1983, fire erupted from an overheated chimney and within a hour Capt. Watson's dream home was gone.

But his name will always been remembered. A lake on the property is called Watson Lake, and at the 108 Heritage site, a popular tourist attraction beside Highway 97, the big log barn he built for his Clydesdale stallions has been faithfully restored. Considered one of the largest barns in Canada, it is a testimony to one man's vision and to a romantic bygone era in Cariboo history.

# Pioneer Churchmen

Whenever I think of Cariboo pioneers, I imagine hardy bearded men driving stagecoaches or freight wagons, hacking a homestead out of forests, or trail driving cattle hundreds of miles to railhead.

But the rigors endured by the first men of the cloth who ministered to the spiritual needs of Williams Lake and the Cariboo-Chilcotin make them worthy of the term "pioneer" and a place in our history.

There are some wonderful tales of their experiences. Rev. Basil A. Resker of St. Peter's Anglican Church in Williams Lake, for instance, was known as "The Fastest Cloak in the West." He had never driven a car before he came to the tiny village in 1926, but over the next twelve years he wore out eight vehicles and clocked 20,000 miles a year covering his vast Cariboo parish.

That record was equalled by Rev. Alex D. MacKinnon of St. Andrew's Presbyterian (later United) Church who arrived in 1921, as well as the frail little priest, Father François Marie Thomas of St. Joseph's Mission, who came from France in 1897 and stayed for almost sixty years.

They travelled thousands of miles on foot, by horseback, buggy or flivver and even snowshoes to carry their message to the people of the Cariboo—preaching in homes, stopping houses, shacks, tents, dance halls and schools, even in the open air, enduring winter's severe cold and the heat of summer under harsh conditions.

Rev. Resker later recalled his early years in Williams Lake in a *Williams Lake Tribune* interview. "There were only 100 people in 1926 and no buildings beyond Second Avenue." At that time the Williams Lake-Chilcotin Mission was the second largest in Canada, so he had an immense territory to cover. He didn't know how to drive, but quickly taught himself on the vacant flats where Safeway is today. There were no driver's tests, so once he had mastered the mechanics he just "took off" for 150 Mile House.

He bought his first car, a Chev Tourer, for $800. "The country roads were terrible. I had chains on all the time when it was wet; you couldn't navigate in the mud otherwise. Lots of sacks and jacks were standard equipment, and in minus 30 degree weather, two buckets were needed—one to drain the oil and one the water. Antifreeze was unknown." He always carried blankets and food as he was often forced to camp out overnight or in a trapper's cabin, and once he spent the night in a haystack.

The vicar often felt he was running a free Cariboo passenger and freight service. "I took people and supplies into ranches, and once even delivered a corpse to Black Creek."

He bounced and rattled over incredibly rough roads to perform baptisms and weddings. He is mentioned in Eric Collier's famed book *"Three Against the Wilderness"* as the itinerant English clergyman who married Eric and Lillian Ross at the Becher House at Riske Creek in September 1928. "He was a roly-poly sort of fellow, short in stature, broad in girth, and as good-humoured and contented as a porcupine sunning itself on a treetop," wrote Collier.

When he was not bashing around the backroads, the little vicar was busy in the village overseeing the building of St. Peter's Anglican Church (the total cost of $4,600 included the site at the corner of Oliver and Third Avenue, considered way out of town then), as well as being involved in community affairs.

Among other things, he formed the First Williams Lake Boy Scout Troop and one of their favourite spots to camp was on a small island in Williams Lake. In fact the lads liked it so much that in 1932, pioneer merchant Roderick Mackenzie, who was MLA for Cariboo then, obtained the provincially-owned island for the village to use as a permanent scout camp. Naturally it then became known as "Scout Island." Today it is part of a complex called the "Scout Island Nature Centre" which includes one of the best migratory bird marshes in the world, a nature house full of wildlife exhibits, as well as many delightful nature trails and a beach.

It must have been with deep regret that the congregation of St. Peter's said good-bye to Rev. Resker in 1938 when he moved to Kimberley. In 1942 he was appointed archdeacon of the Kootenays, and later retired to Nelson where he died in 1969.

*A man of immense energy, Reverend Basil Resker stands amid his scouts. The pristine island in Williams Lake was a frequent destination for the troop's campouts. The tiny village of Williams Lake can be seen in the background. (1934 photo courtesy of RCAF) The scouts are left to right, standing: Tommy Thomas, Dunc Taylor, Victor Gaspard, Jack Hodgson, Joe Rickard, Scoutmaster Resker, Joe Smith, Raymond Wise, Harry Taylor, Sid Pigeon, Percy Pigeon. Front Row: Gordon Elliott, Bernard Beasley, Gordon Jakel, Wilfred Hodgson, Herb Barber, Bob Spencer, Billy Smith.*

Today the lovely little St. Peter's Anglican Church, which was moved to Carson Drive in 1957, is the oldest remaining church in Williams Lake.

Rev. Alex MacKinnon, a big rosy-cheeked Nova Scotian, known to his friends simply as "A.D.," arrived in 1921 to become Williams Lake's first minister. Like Resker he travelled a circuit which extended 300 miles east and west, 100 miles north and south, visiting lonely log cabins and holding divine service wherever a group could

*On Easter morning, 1923, Reverend Alex MacKinnon stands erect (upper left) in front of Williams Lake's new church on Oliver Street with members of his congregation and a Sunday School blessed by bows and beaming faces.*

be gathered. I have a faded photo of the minister using a stump as a pulpit at an open air service at Black Creek in 1930.

In later years MacKinnon would recall preaching at Lone Butte "where the services were held in the open air, and the most hardy souls climbed up the cliff and sang the hymns from the high pinnacle."

The good minister took many hazardous trips into the wilderness, sometimes sliding off the road, or walking miles in subzero temperatures, and even getting lost with his wife on a trip back from Beaver Valley. They were not found for twenty-four hours, and everybody for miles around flocked to hear his sermon the following Sunday on "Thoughts and Feelings While Lost in the Bush."

St. Andrew's Presbyterian Church, built on Oliver Street in 1922, was Williams Lake's first church, and until Rev. Resker arrived, the Anglicans worshipped there too. Rev. MacKinnon was also one of the "movers and shakers" in local politics and was president of the Board of Trade, Hospital Board, Stampede Association, Fall Fair, and Farmers' Institute. Not only that, but when Williams Lake was incorporated as a village in 1929, he was one of three interim commissioners named to organize the new municipality.

Although Rev. MacKinnon played a big part in early Williams Lake history, it was his two daughters, Joy and Lovette, who really grabbed the spotlight.

The two little girls learned to skate on a frog pond near the back door of the manse, then later, while attending high school in Vancouver they took skating lessons and were spotted by a British theatrical company. Asked to join their troupe of outstanding skaters of the Empire, exhibitions followed in Canada, the United States, Africa, Australia, and Europe capped by a command performance for British royalty in London.

On one of their trips back to Williams Lake, the sisters performed for hometown crowds on the open air rink near the present day Safeway store. Local resident Margaret Elliott recalled the scene:

*Although the town's first boarded rink was a hockey haven in the 1920s (the current city hall now stands where the old hospital is seen atop the knoll) one of its biggest crowds came to the home-coming of the world famous MacKinnon sisters. Lovette (left) and Joy were twin apples of their father's eye.*

The evening was mild, rink lights glistened on the ice, and a phonograph wheezed out the 'Skater's Waltz' as we lined the board fence around the rink, ten deep, chatting and waiting in happy anticipation.

Out came the two charming girls. Dressed in gay skating costumes, they swirled, twirled and whirled in intricate spins in grace and beauty unexcelled.

Gently it began to snow. The whole scene turned into a veritable fairyland, a storybook picture. Although we chafed our hands and stamped our feet to keep warm, we would gladly have watched all night. Larger and thicker came the snowflakes. Whiter and deeper became the snow on the gay crowd, veiling the skaters until it became too deep for them to continue.

Happily we trudged home in the snowstorm after a most memorable evening.

But eventually the dazzling MacKinnon sisters split up. On a second tour of Australia, Lovette met and married Lord Arthur Percy de Villiers and gave up her career. With another partner, Joy continued to skate professionally and in 1941 joined the famous Ice Capades and for the next four years toured the U.S. In 1946 she married a captain in the U.S. Army Air Force, and presumably gave up her career also.

When Rev. MacKinnon left Williams Lake in 1941 after dedicating twenty years to the village and its people, he finished the last of his fifty years in the ministry at Peachland before returning to Nova Scotia where he died in 1949. But when the present St. Andrew's United Church in Williams Lake was built in 1982, their first pastor was not forgotten and the new auditorium was thoughtfully named "MacKinnon Hall."

Both of these pioneer churchmen are remembered in Williams Lake streets which bear their names—MacKinnon Street and Resker Place.

Father Thomas, the last of this trio of dedicated churchmen, was a truly remarkable man. Born in Brittany, France, his health, even in his youth, was poor. He almost died of typhoid fever and was threatened with tuberculosis, but nothing would deter him from his desired vocation and in 1888 he joined the Oblates of Mary Immaculate. The young priest was given the choice of staying in Brittany rather than risk his life in a raw new country, but he chose to come to British Columbia and eventually the Cariboo.

*Pictured here in the 1800s, St Joseph's Mission and Industrial School near Williams Lake was Father Thomas's home for six decades while he served his church and preached their gospel over almost 200,000 square kilometers. One of the good father's final requests was to be buried in the Cariboo. (Photo courtesy Irene Stangoe)*

*Father Thomas travelled around his far-flung parish in a crude wooden sleigh visiting settlers and the various Chilcotin reserves over a period of six decades. (Photo courtesy John Roberts)*

Posted to St. Joseph's Mission near Williams Lake in the spring of 1897, he stayed for almost sixty years, a familiar yet impressive black bearded figure in his black cassock as he administered to whites and natives alike in a mission territory which covered from Prince George to Clinton, from Horsefly to the Coast Range in the Chilcotin.

An article in *Oblate Missions'* spring issue of 1957 tells of the hardships he suffered in early years,

> The food was coarse and often uncooked; for years his diet consisted of bacon, beans, dried beef, and frozen fish. There were the rigors of travel by horse and sleigh; he often rode from four in the morning until ten at night.

> And there was the cold. It was not uncommon for the wine to freeze in the chalice in some of the icy chapels when the temperature sank to 40 or 50 below and the wind driven snow swirled through great cracks in the log walls.

> Sleep often meant curling up under some wagon or on the rough plank floor of a cabin; then there were the lice . . . and the blood thirsty mosquitoes.

His narrow escapes from death or injury were so frequent that a fellow priest claimed "he must have had a dozen guardian angels."

Father Thomas was not the first of the Oblate Fathers to come to the Cariboo-Chilcotin, but he stayed the longest. Quite stern and rigid in his beliefs, he was nevertheless highly respected and loved, especially among his Indian charges. For the last thirty years of his ministry, he concentrated on the plateau west of Williams Lake and became known as the "Apostle of the Chilcotin."

Oblate brothers and priests who die in the west are normally buried in the cemetery of St. Mary's Mission at Mission City, but when Father Thomas died in an Edmonton hospital in his 89th year, an exception was made. At his request, he was brought back to the Cariboo he loved and buried in the little cemetery at St. Joseph's Mission. Hundreds of people attended his funeral, with natives from Sugar Cane, Soda Creek, Canim Lake, Alkali Lake, and throughout the Chilcotin following the procession, praying aloud in their own language as they walked, saying the very prayers which Father Thomas had taught them.

# Everything From
## Cheese to Dynamite

Roderick Mackenzie and his partner John Fraser must have been pretty devastated when their store, the first one in the new village of Williams Lake, burned to the ground and two young men lost their lives in the blaze.

The fire broke out on 10 July, 1921. In those early years, the weekly "train day" was a big event, and everyone rushed down to the PGE depot to get in on the excitement. On that Sunday afternoon, a young girl was using a gas iron in the apartment above the Fraser & Mackenzie store on Railway Avenue and unfortunately left it burning when she dashed over to the station. Soon the entire store was ablaze, with the flames quickly spreading to the Lakeview Hotel, Elliott's Meat Market, and Herb Spencer's dance hall.

"In forty minutes they were all flat," said longtime resident Laura Moxon who many years later recalled the terrifying scene as the four rough frame buildings collapsed one by one, wiping out half the business district. Little was saved, although willing hands helped postmaster Claude Dodwell carry mailsacks out of the post office in the store.

Johnny Salmon and Bernard Weetman were among those trying to salvage the mail, and in the confusion it was not until Monday afternoon that friends realized they were missing. A search of the ruins soon revealed the grisly truth. The second storey had collapsed trapping the two men below, and their bodies were found side by side, charred beyond recognition. They were buried in the little cemetery at St. Joseph's Mission south of Williams Lake.

Despite the tragedy, Fraser and Mackenzie quickly rebuilt. Little is known about Fraser, but Mackenzie was a man born with a strong pioneering spirit which had taken him from the highlands of Scotland and halfway around the globe before finding his niche in the raw Cariboo cattle country.

He first apprenticed to a merchandising firm in Glasgow, then London, before voyaging to South Africa to work for a German firm. Early in his career the young clerk was faced with his first big sales problem when a mistake was made in his order from England. How do you manage to sell twenty billiard tables to homesteaders in the remote regions of the Transvaal when they are expecting dining room tables?

*Rod Mackenzie, pioneer merchant came to Williams Lake in 1919.*

The error didn't faze the canny enterprising Scot, however, and he boldly set out, selling them at double the profit the tables would have brought.

After serving with a Highland regiment during the Boer War, Mackenzie went into business for himself, but new frontiers were beckoning, and in 1910 he was off for Canada and Vancouver with his wife and family. At that time the provincial government was again talking of pushing the Pacific Great Eastern Railway into the interior, with Squamish envisioned as an important deep sea port, so it was not surprising that Mackenzie chose this spot for his first store.

The dream for Squamish's future never became a reality, but Mackenzie's store there, at the beginning of the PGE line, prospered. (Until 1956 travellers had to go by Union steamship from North Vancouver to Squamish, then board the train.)

Progress on the PGE was slow, very slow. Beset with problems within the company and the outbreak of World War I, the line had been completed only as far as Lone Butte by 1919, but down in Squamish the adventurous Scot with itchy feet decided to follow the ribbon of steel into the Interior. From Lone Butte, he walked most of the way up the rough rutted Cariboo Wagon Road until he got to the proposed new village of Williams Lake.

There was practically nothing on the bare hillsides—just a cluster of shacks and tents and the big Borland/Pinchbeck house set in the

*Possibly Rod Mackenzie's biggest coup was gaining the Cariboo's first liquor outlet after B.C.'s prohibition ended in the 1920s. He proved himself an astute merchandiser on three continents. That's Charlie Mulvahill at the reins of his six-horse team pulling away with a wagon-load of supplies for his Chezacut ranch in the Chilcotin.*

natural amphitheatre that would later become the Stampede grounds. But at the townsite he found great excitement as sweating crews inched the rails around the lake, and surveyors were laying out the new streets.

Did Mackenzie foresee that one day Williams Lake would be the "cattle capital of B.C.," shipping more beef than any other area in the province? Certainly he envisioned great things for this divisional point on the PGE, and quickly picked a site for his store on Railway Avenue opposite the proposed depot. His store was the first permanent building in the tiny village. His partner, John Fraser of Squamish, moved to Williams Lake to manage the new venture called Fraser & Mackenzie, General Merchants, handling "everything from cheese to dynamite."

The new store aptly enough was also termed "The Big Store" which brings me around to a funny story Rod loved to tell on himself. After he returned to his Squamish store, a salesman travelling through remarked to Mackenzie about the fine prospects in Squamish, then commented "but you should see the big box of a thing some guy is building in Williams Lake."

From the beginning Mackenzie was determined to compete with the Harvey Bailey Co. store at Ashcroft. Up to this time, Cariboo-Chilcotin ranchers had had to trail drive their cattle the long grueling miles to the CPR railhead there, and also buy their yearly supplies. Now with cattlemen able to ship by PGE from Williams Lake, it was a different story. By 1920 Williams Lake was booming and the town was a scene of wild confusion as merchants goaded contractors and workmen to greater efforts so they could get into operation and reap the rewards.

There were no police (except for Sgt. Gallagher, who rode up from 150 Mile House periodically), no licensed premises or bar, but several excellent bootleggers like "One-Arm McLean" who imported stock from Alberta. "We danced every night in the Fraser Mackenzie store," remembered one resident. "There was nothing else to do."

It was amazing how quickly the little village grew. Soon there were three hotels, two banks, the T. A. Moore general store, a church, a couple of restaurants, a barber, and a blacksmith who was the busiest man in town. When it rained it took a team of five horses to pull a load up Oliver Street. One wag opined that the mud was so bad "even in a heavy dew you could hardly stand up."

The big fire of 1921 did not stop the momentum, and soon a row of buildings again faced Railway Avenue and business carried on. When Fraser & Mackenzie rebuilt, they snagged the licence for the first liquor outlet, thus ending prohibition and bringing more business to the Big Store.  In 1924 when Fraser retired, Mackenzie bought out his partner's interest, and moved to Williams Lake to take over the active management of the store which then became known simply as "Mackenzies' Ltd."

## Mackenzies' Mining Camp
### and Prospectors' Supplies.

| | |
|---|---|
| Repel-It Waterproof Pants, per pair | $ 3.35 |
| "      "      Shirts, each | 3.85 |
| "      "      Breeches, per pair | 3.85 |
| Cruiser Waterproof Shirts, each | 6.25 |
| Hunting Coats, each | 7.00 |
| Dry Bak Hats, each | 1.35 |
| Stanfield's Red Label Shirts and Drawers, each | 2.15 |
| Caribou brand Overalls, 30 to 44, per pair | 1,45 |
| Jumbo Sweaters, all wool, shawl collar, each | 3.00 |
| Gold Pan, each, 50c and | ,75 |
| Prospectors' Picks, each | 2.00 |
| Half Axe, each | 1.60 |
| Sheath Knife, each | 2.00 |

Also Fry Pans, Coffee and Tea Pots, Hudson Bay Kettles, etc.

## Mackenzies Ltd.
#### The Mail Order House of the Cariboo.

*1930s advertisement in the* Williams Lake Tribune.

From then on Rod Mackenzie was a formidable force in the Cariboo and the town's most dominant personality. A crusty, stern employer who demanded a good day's work and could be hard as steel in business dealings, he also was openhanded to those in need. During the 1930s, when the price of beef sank to two cents a pound, Mackenzie strained his credit to the utmost to help the ranchers so they could weather the Depression. He barely made it himself.

For many years Mackenzie took a leading role in town and district affairs, and from 1928 to 1932 served as Conservative MLA for the Cariboo district. His political campaigning gave rise to some humorous stories. On one junket to Lillooet the shrewd Scot decided to take along a load of dynamite on his truck. His daughter Anne (Stevenson) went along too, and his political opponents used the incident to call down Mackenzie as "being so stingy he makes his daughter ride on the load."

Ever the visionary, he quickly established a store at Wells near Barkerville, with son Jack as manager, when the Cariboo Gold Quartz mine was discovered there in 1932. He sold in 1950, but still kept the Squamish store which in later years was owned by son Alistair.

Even after retirement this rugged hardy man was still playing golf, took up curling in his 80s, and thought nothing of driving out to Likely with a load of gyproc, or dashing down to see how things were in Squamish. Some of the stories of Mackenzie's exploits behind the wheel are unbelievably funny, others downright scary. He appeared to use the same "damn the torpedoes, full steam ahead" in driving that had characterized his life since he left Scotland.

In 1956 the street in front of his store was changed from Railway to Mackenzie Avenue in honour of this grand old pioneer of Williams Lake. He died just a year later, in April 1957, just a month or so after his wife Elizabeth. She too had endured her share of hardships while following her husband to South Africa, then Squamish, before putting down roots in the Cariboo.

In 1968 Roderick Mackenzie's pioneer store, along with the large grocery department he added in 1946, was purchased by Fields Ltd. who later boarded up the old section.

On Boxing Day, 1996 the end came for the Big Store when a major conflagration wiped out Fields Ltd. including the empty Fraser & Mackenzie store, as well as the Ranch Hotel, formerly the Log Cabin Hotel built in 1920.

Gone was over 75 years of Williams Lake history.

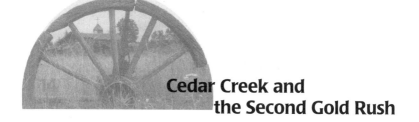

# Cedar Creek and
# the Second Gold Rush

"Williams Lake, City of Tents" read the banner headline on the front page of a Vancouver daily paper in May 1922. Behind the headline was the story of the Cariboo's second gold rush, 63 years after men first came into the country searching for the yellow metal.

This time the rush was concentrated at Cedar Creek, three miles from Likely, and the newly created village of Williams Lake was the jumping off place for the new discovery.

The rush was triggered by the incredible find of two prospectors—a grizzled old miner by the name of Alfred A. Platt and his partner, young Johnny Lyne, the blacksmith at the 150 Mile House. Acting on the advice of old John Likely who claimed that Cedar Creek's "mother lode" had never been found, the two men began laboriously working the canyon benches of the ten-mile-long creek in August 1921.

Three months later, discouraged and ready to quit, they were on top of Warren Mountain when Platt stopped at a small reed choked water hole to get a drink. Noticing traces of colour, he scooped up the gravel and to his amazement found gold nuggets gleaming in his hands.

He leaped to his feet and shouted to Lyne, who thought his partner was having a fit as he mouthed almost incoherent words and pointed to the pond. But before going out to register their claims, Platt made two mistakes which cost the partners a small fortune. First he placed his staking lines in a half moon along the top of the gulch, then he dropped off a note to a trapper friend on Quesnel Lake.

*The Cedar Creek gold rush was a boom for fledgling Williams Lake. Here, in 1925, Gus Jakel (right) ties a load of pipe destined for the gold camp to his two-year-old Ruggles truck while sidekick, Tommy Mart, shows more interest in the camera.*

*Cedar Creek Placer Operations. (BCARS D-04758)*

*This monolith of past industry, remnant of Likely's Bullion Mine, now sits in Cedar Creek Park.(*Williams Lake Tribune *photo)*

Before spring, six trappers staked claims around the discovery, and the rush was on. When surveyors came in, they struck a straight line from Platt's starting point, and the "Glory Hole"—the very rich shaft from which the majority of the gold would come—was on the neighbouring claim of Ed Stevens, one of the six trappers. Platt and Lyne ended up with only one percent of their original strike.

During its peak in 1922, it was estimated that 7,000 men flocked to Cedar Creek and this time Williams Lake was the centre of the unexpected boom.

Roland Goodchild was among those eager men who rushed north to try their luck in the new diggings. "I arrived in Williams Lake on March 13, 1922," he wrote, "and found it even then full of early arrivals, all looking for teams to get their outfits to Cedar Creek.

"Williams Lake boasted three stores, two hotels, a few log barns, the PGE depot, and not much else. Rooms were at a premium, and tents were pitched along the railway. The side road to Quesnel Dam (later renamed Likely) was little more than an overgrown trail."

Williams Lake old timer Ben Clarke also remembered that "with the gold seekers came two other hordes, lawyers and journalists. It seemed for awhile that every tent and shack bore the sign of a law firm, and even the school teacher put out his shingle as a 'legal adviser.' "

Goodchild left Williams Lake on one of the two last sleighs. "At the Indian village north of the lake (Sugar Cane), one sleigh broke down under the enormous strain of 7,000 pounds of freight; the other stuck in a mud hole on the side of a hill.

"The thermometer had dropped to ten below zero. I commenced to walk to the 150 Mile House five miles distant with my typewriter on my back. The trail was bare though as slippery as glass and uphill all the way. Many were making the 65-mile trip on foot with their outfits on their backs."

After three days of appalling travel, Goodchild finally got to the Cedar Creek camp. Shacks were being erected, he wrote, a store was in operation, tents were pitched along the lake, and shafts were being sunk all over the place.

Goodchild commented that the camp was neat and orderly, although the police had relieved one or two wild spirits of their six shooters. But it was not always so quiet. Other reports say there was a great deal of bootlegging, and in the spring of 1923, twelve provincial police arrived and on a sudden Saturday night raid manacled eighty-three men and women to trees.

The strike at Cedar Creek did not go smoothly; claims were taken over by promoters who sold millions of "units" which amounted to worthless shares. Hijacking was rife. Many of the men who flocked to Cedar Creek found the paying ground staked, and left in disgust.

Thus the Cariboo's second gold rush died almost as quickly as it was born. The Cariboo Mining Company eventually acquired most of the claims for $4,000 and continued to work there until 1938. The last company ceased operations in 1952. The Cedar Creek area was believed to have yielded over $5,000,000 in gold.

And what of the two discoverers?

A year after the fabulous find, Platt died in a taxicab in Prince George of a heart attack. Lyne continued to live at Williams Lake, and was over ninety when he died—still philosophically maintaining that it was just as well he did not get all that money.

No story of Cedar Creek would be complete without the mention of the indomitable Barney Boe of Williams Lake. Born in Norway, he emigrated to the U.S. in 1901 and eventually found his way to Vancouver where he established a plumbing and heating firm. But he fell in love with the Cariboo and in the early 1920s also opened a business in Williams Lake, and acquired a gold mine at Cedar Creek.

Among Barney's many exploits was the purchase of a plane in 1930 so he could commute more easily between Cedar Creek, Williams Lake and Vancouver. He taught himself to fly and over the next sixteen years logged thousands of miles in his small aircraft.

*Barney Boe, the Cariboo's most durable bush pilot, celebrated his 100th birthday in 1987 with a best friend. Plumbing contractor, goldminer, and self-taught pilot, Barney used Williams Lake as his home base.* (William's Lake Tribune *photo*)

During World War II he installed heating systems in army and air force camps, flying in and out of remote areas overseeing his crews.

He was almost sixty years old, one of the oldest civilians still flying, when he sold his plane in 1946. After several owners, it was acquired in 1961 by the Provincial Museum at Victoria and now hangs in the magnificent Clifford Carl Hall, formerly the main entrance, as a striking example of the many bush planes and their daring pilots who opened up remote areas of B.C., the Yukon and Alaska.

*In 1994 Barney Boe's CF-AOD registered plane was mounted in Victoria's Royal B.C. Museum as a fitting monument to B.C.'s pioneer bush pilots. (Photo courtesy Royal British Columbia Museum)*

Barney mined his claim at Cedar Creek for many years, and a 1929 news item in the *Province* headlined "Gets $10,000 in Gold Mine" relates how Barney had arrived in the city with 500 ounces in gold from his diggings. But it eventually petered out.

The 1921 strike at Cedar Creek was not the first. Gold was found there as early as 1859 during the original rush to the Cariboo, although James Edwards is generally credited with making the first real discovery in 1861. A small community optimistically called "Cedar City" sprang up. There was a store, butcher shop, saloon, about fifty miners' cabins, and a hotel partially built when the entire settlement was destroyed by fire in 1869.

Chinese and Welsh miners continued to placer mine the lower portion of Cedar Creek, and took out a few thousand in gold annually, but apparently did not follow the creek to its source, nor find the rich deposit discovered many years later by Platt and Lyne.

Ironically, in that mining is often blamed for environmental damage, it was the tailings and flumes left by these miners that saved the stand of beautiful cedars on the shores of Quesnel Lake. Believed to be over 1,000 years old when the great fire of 1869 swept through the Cariboo, taking everything in its path, these trees were spared by the rocky graveyard of tailings. The trees are now enshrined in Cedar Creek Park, thanks to the efforts of Capt. Norman Evans-Atkinson, another early adventurer, who came to try his luck during the 1921-22 rush, and stayed. For years the captain battled to save the majestic trees, and finally in 1962 his dream came true when the government set aside Cedar Creek Point for a park.

Another major point of interest in the park is a huge steam shovel, one of the "Twin Giants" brought into the country at the turn of the century by John Hobson, manager of the famous Bullion Mine near Likely. When it ceased operations in 1941, the Bullion was the largest hydraulic operation in the world; had dug the largest man made gash (the Vancouver Hotel would be lost in this hole), and used the largest monitors (i.e. huge water cannons, thirty feet long, which sprayed the hillside with tremendous force, washing down the gravel which hopefully would bear gold).

The massive shovels were used to dig a ditch and right-of-way from Spanish Lake to the mine, but the project was abandoned due to financial troubles. Evans-Atkinson and the Likely Chamber of Commerce got one of the old derelicts moved five miles to Cedar Point Park in 1962, thus preserving another bit of history for generations to come.

It should be noted, however, that there's still gold in them thar hills, or rather, "pit." The Bullion Mine was reopened in 1993 and has been operating off-and-on since then. The owners hope that one day they will strike another "mother lode."

# The Longest Town
# in the Cariboo

Axes, potlatches, camels, and skating down fish–these all make for intriguing reading when you delve into the history of Lac la Hache. As many of you know, the name translated means "Lake of the Axe," but its exact origin appears to be lost in the mists of time. There seems no doubt, however, that it was named by the French-Canadian *voyageurs* who paddled the rivers and trod the brigade trails of the Cariboo carrying furs to and from Hudson's Bay forts.

But did one of those early *coureurs de bois* lose his axe when they made camp beside the gleaming waters, or did he find one?

Both versions can be found in historical articles, but Lac la Hache historian Molly Forbes, 96, favours the story handed down by the McKinlay family, the first settlers in the valley, in which a *voyageur* made the "grim discovery" of a small axe by the shores of the lovely lake. Could it have been a hatchet lost by the native people who,

*Mr. and Mrs. McKinlay*

long before the white man came into the country, had a thriving village on its shores? They called the beautiful twelve-mile lake "Kumatakwa" or Queen of the Waters.

An important chapter of Cariboo history was written at Lac la Hache. At the annual Indian games and potlatch in 1859, Chief Anaham, fiery old chief of the Chilcotins, was all for war with the white men who were pushing north in their search for gold. But the counsel of Chief William of the Williams Lake Indian Band convinced the assembled natives to welcome them "in a spirit of friendship and goodwill."

At that same potlatch Peter Dunlevy and his eager band of prospectors first met Baptiste, the native guide who would lead them to the Horsefly River where they made the first major strike in the Cariboo, triggering the great Cariboo gold rush.

As men poured up the Cariboo Wagon Road built in 1862-5 to give access to the fabulous gold fields at Barkerville, the pioneering families of Archibald McKinlay, Isaac Ogden, and Gavin Hamilton settled in the Lac la Hache area with McKinlay's 115 Mile House as well as the 122 Mile House becoming stopping places for the BX Express.

Freight teams, stagecoaches, wagons, men on foot and yes, even camels passed by their doors.

*122 Mile House was a classic Cariboo roadhouse operated by George Forbes and his family after 1893. Like many such houses it evolved from a BX stop where fresh horses were kept ready for the frequent changes needed by the stagecoaches and their drivers. (Photo courtesy Molly Forbes)*

*Given the oddity of camels along the Cariboo road it is surprising that more photos of the beasts haven't survived. This famous photo has often been used to document their existence.*

The ill-fated attempt to use camels as pack animals to the Cariboo gold fields was triggered by an advertisement in the Victoria *Colonist* in March 1862 offering twenty-five camels for sale in San Francisco. A syndicate headed by Frank Laumeister of Victoria knew that camels had been used with some success by the U.S. Army in Texas and California, and figured they would work well in the Cariboo. After all, the camel could carry 1,000 pounds compared to 400 pounds for a mule, and could travel 30 to 40 miles a day on little food or water.

But the rocky trails of the Cariboo proved unsuitable for the camel's tender feet, which were accustomed to sand. And then there was his smell. The stench from the strange ill-humoured beasts was so strong that other pack animals on the trails went wild whenever the camels were in the vicinity. This resulted in several serious accidents which brought lawsuits against Laumeister, and his company almost went broke over the whole unfortunate experience.

Most of the camels were turned loose on the range east of the North Thompson River to spend their declining years, but in a story published in the Vancouver *Province* in 1926, pioneer stagecoach driver Frank Leighton declared that he saw several in the Lac la Hache valley near the 114 Mile post in 1865 while on his way to Barkerville.

Yet another item, source unknown, says five to eight camels died in a heavy snowstorm there one winter and were buried at the 117 Mile where a wooden headboard describing their history was erected. Today nothing can be found, but I can't help but wonder what an archaeologist would think if he dug up the bones of a half a dozen camels in the Cariboo 1,000 years from now.

As an exit to the great Cariboo camel misadventure, I should tell you the humorous legend of how Adler & Barry, the enterprising proprietors of the 150 Mile roadhouse and saloon allegedly purchased a camel in the summer of 1863, butchered it and attempted to serve "camel mulligan" to their patrons. Apparently their customers were not amused and refused to partake of the delicacy.

Like so many of the stopping places along the Cariboo Road, Lac la Hache gradually dwindled in importance with the advent of cars but even then it still managed to attract attention one way or another.

People often look skeptical when you mention how they used to "skate down fish" on Lac la Hache, but it is a true story. Believed to have been introduced by the French-Canadians, it was an exciting but dangerous sport and over the years two men have lost their lives when they plunged through thin ice into the frigid waters—Archie Nicholson in 1928, and Reginald Sinclair of Victoria in 1956.

But Molly Forbes, who was only twenty-eight when the accompanying photos were taken, doesn't remember being a bit scared. "We always carried an axe to test the ice," she explained. "If the axe went flying through, you knew it was not safe." Duncan McKinlay was still skating down fish when he was in his 70s, she says.

Conditions had to be just right to be successful in skating down and spearing the big char which could weigh up to twenty pounds. And it could only happen in the fall when the lake first froze over. The ice then is only 1 1/2 inches thick, very thin and clear, and rather rubbery, which explains why skating down fish is dangerous.

The little kokanee salmon, for which Lac la Hache is famous, would come in near the shoreline to feed during the night, and the char would follow them in.

In early morning the skaters would be out, hoping to catch sight of the char through the crystal clear ice and the race would be on. While one or two drove the fish into more shallow water, the last member of the party chopped a hole through the ice some distance in front of the fish. Then as the char slowly passed the hole, it was speared or gaffed.

Spearing Fish -- 20 Lbs Landed
Forbes' Ranch - 122 Mile House
Lac La Hache, B. C.

"You had to be a really fast skater," says Molly, "and really fast too in chopping the hole, or with a flash the big char would be gone." Once the first snowfall came, the sport ended. Today, it is illegal to spear any game fish, so another little bit of Lac la Hache history has died.

Another sport which made history at Lac la Hache was horse racing. "The race track was right down the middle of the village on the Cariboo Road," says Molly, "and they raced from the 117 Mile down to the 115."

This was before Williams Lake and its famous stampede came into existence in 1919. Lac la Hache then was the big social center of the Cariboo and its rodeo or "potlatches" brought people from as far away as Kamloops. The hillsides were covered with tents, and the celebrations went on for a whole week. There was no steer riding or bronc riding as in today's rodeos; just foot races, wrestling, horse racing, dancing every night, and the sounds of natives playing Lahal—a game of wits, ceremonial endurance and chance. The Lac la Hache races gradually petered out, says Molly, after Williams Lake came into being and "took all the glory" with their stampede.

Today Lac la Hache still clings to fame with their boast of being "The Longest Town in the Cariboo." Certainly it is long on history.

*In the 1930s, 28 year-old Molly Forbes watches husband Gilbert (right) and Archie MacDougall nab a beauty. A gaffing spear was used to reap the catch after the fish were chased into shallow water. (Photo courtesy Molly Forbes)*

# Remembering
## One Room Schools

## The Girl in the Grey Cardboard Box

The school inspector referred to the new teacher as "The Girl in the Grey Cardboard Box," an apt description of her Riske Creek accommodation that the young woman didn't mind a bit.

The year was 1938 and times were tough, so when Barbara (Reid) Buckley was offered a chance to teach at the remote little school, she jumped at it. Barbara boarded with Bob and Anna French who had been persuaded to take in the teacher, even though they had four children and only a two-room log house. They set up a bed on one side of the main room, and partitioned it off with grey building paper to give her privacy—hence the inspector's humorous comment.

"But the house was spotless and I was the honoured guest," Barbara recalled in her memoirs. She had the only chair while Bob and the children sat on benches and Anna on an apple box.

"I thought the stories of using Eaton's catalogue as toilet paper were fairy tales, but it was a fact of life in the Chilcotin. The catalogue had a string threaded through the spine and hung on a nail. When I went home to Vancouver at Christmas, I saved Mandarin orange papers and brought them back to add a more civilized touch to the old outhouse."

The school was a small sod-roofed log building. It was supposed to have been freshly chinked with mud, but that had not been done. "When I arrived you could see daylight through many of the wide cracks," Barbara related. The usual potbellied stove provided heat. Desks, a blackboard, a bench for the drinking water pail, and a row of large nails hammered into a back log for the children's coats made up the furnishings. "There were absolutely no frills, not even a single library book. My total year's supply from the school board was a bottle of ink and a box of chalk."

Women were scarce in the Chilcotin, so the school marm was a matrimonial catch. "All the unattached males, young and old, came to size me up," she recalls. She also met Jerry Buckley, "a big good-hearted Irishman" who ranched just five miles away and, as it turned out, would become a permanent part of her life.

In November Anna informed her that the teacher always gave a dance to raise money for the kids' Christmas party. "But what about music?" Barbara protested. There was no piano, no record player, not even a radio in the school. "There are musicians around," Anna replied calmly. "Dick Stowell and Eric Collier play the fiddle."

The school was so dingy with dusty logs and the ever chipping, mud-filled cracks that Barbara sent a frantic SOS to her mother for rolls of green and red crepe paper to make decorations.

Then the big night arrived. "The women brought refreshments and children. The men brought trucks, horses, and booze," Barbara wrote. "The bottles were hidden outside in the woodpile and needless to say there were numerous trips to get wood." The dance was peaceful and a great success. "Small babies and tired children slept

*The Riske Creek student body in the late 1930s included the Jasper clan in the back row (l to r) Delmer, Mary, June, Wesley, and Gordon and in the front row Walter Stobie, Marie French, Willie Hurst, Bobby French, and Jack Renner. (Photo courtesy June Bliss)*

on the benches, the inebriated were tucked underneath, and the last of the crowd did not leave until daybreak."

It was a desperately cold winter with temperatures dropping down to thirty-five and forty below for six straight weeks. "The snow was like a covering of diamonds against the blue sky. Occasionally the stillness would be broken by a sound like a rifle shot when a tree or telephone pole would split with the intense cold."

Travellers on the Chilcotin road were few and far between in those days, Barbara relates, and only once or twice a day did a car go by. "In the spring we could only travel on the frost at about 2:00 a.m. In the daytime, the road was a sea of mud."

Barbara also learned to ride "on a Model T horse with the cunning of a fox," and spent an exhausting but exhilarating weekend working on a spring roundup. As summer neared, the French family decided to move to Alexis Creek, so without their children the Riske Creek school had to close. In June the young teacher left too, but returned a year later as Mrs. Jerry Buckley and embarked on another adventure as the wife of a Cariboo rancher.

## Marmots and the Enterprise School

Another young woman who taught in a one-room Cariboo-Chilcotin school during the Dirty Thirties was Ilma (Beamish) Dunn of White Rock. It was a beautiful sunny day 3 September, 1932, when Ilma walked up the Cariboo Highway to get her first glimpse of the one-room Enterprise School where she would be teaching for the next year.

"My heart sank when I saw its condition. The door was ajar and little marmots had made it their home over the summer. Piles of their droppings were in the corner, and the place had a terrible smell. I sat down at the low table which passed for the teacher's desk and cried . . ."

When I first read of Ilma's teaching experiences in an article she wrote for the 1989 fall issue of the *B.C. Historical News*, I immediately thought she was referring to the abandoned log school and its lopsided stile that is such a familiar sight today on Highway 97 near the 132 Mile House and the Enterprise Road. (*See Cariboo-Chilcotin, Pioneer People & Places*.) But not so, I discovered. There was another Enterprise School near the 140 Mile which I never knew existed.

*"Enterprise School, Fall of 1932 after the new flag pole was put up" and "I was proud of my little school" wrote Ilma Beamish on the back of these photos taken at Enterprise. (Ilma Dunn photo)*

"Schools were hard to come by in the 1930s," wrote Ilma. There were dozens of applications for every vacancy and she considered herself "one of the lucky ones" despite the condition of her school. Not only had the marmots made it their home, but it was dark and badly in need of painting. The roof leaked and there was only one outside toilet, rated "poor" by the inspector.

Ilma boarded with the Clem Wright family at the 137 Mile House, and Clem and his hired help cleaned and repaired the school, provided a flagpole for the Union Jack, which by law had to be raised and lowered each school day, and donated a sheep for her to raffle. With the proceeds, she purchased a proper teacher's desk, a bell, and other requirements.

Each morning she would walk the two and a half miles to school. "There was always plenty of wildlife to be seen. The little marmots would pop in and out of their holes, and I loved to listen to them whistle to their mates telling them an intruder was around. In the spring I remember how the saucy little northern bluebirds would hop from post to post on the rail fence that lined the highway and in winter moose and deer would join with the cattle at their feeding stations in the fields."

*Ilma poses with stage driver Clarence Stephenson in Ashcroft, Easter 1933. (Ilma Dunn photo)*

Ilma had just eight students in Grades 1, 3, 5 and 7—four LaBounty and four Wright children, with Jack Wright being the biggest and best helper. "He and Doug Wright looked after bringing in the water each morning from the well, and kept the wood box full for the upright stove. I made the fire each morning and heated water for lunchtime cocoa with lots of fresh cream from the 137 to go with it."

The LaBounty children drove the thirteen miles to school in a little two-wheeled cart which in winter was equipped with runners. Jack and Doug Wright rode horseback with Kathleen and Phyllis riding behind.

"My year at the 137 Mile House was one of the happiest of my life," writes Ilma. She learned to play bridge and 500, went crosscountry skiing, on hayrides, and to country dances. She often came up to Williams Lake, and recalls a win-ter trip with Maggie Hamilton to watch her brother play hockey in the only rink, an outdoor one. "To watch and cheer for your favourite team in the bitter cold was almost a hardship."

*The LaBounty cart carried Herbie, Lila, Raymond and Irwin thirteen miles to the Enterprise classroom. (Ilma Dunn photo)*

Her article is peppered with anecdotes of a fabulous turkey dinner at Crosina's 153 Mile stopping house and the frivolity that went on until the wee hours; and of Clarence Stephenson, amiable owner/driver of the IT Coach Line, who would offer her a ride to school if there was room, and entertained passengers with tales of BX stagecoach days.

Then there was the story of the Felker ghost at the 144 Mile house. William Phillip Felker, the son of pioneer ranchers George and Antoinette Felker, died  in an upstairs bedroom of the historic house after a lengthy battle with cancer.

"In life he claimed he would come back," relates Ilma, "and every morning he did, lighting the fire in the kitchen stove, then sitting down in the rocking chair beside it. How could we not believe when many others had seen the mysterious rocking chair, heard the crackling fire and felt the ghostly presence?"

Ilma travelled to the Cariboo on that September day in 1932 on the PGE railway (now B.C. Rail) and got off at the tiny Enterprise Station. At that time there was a depot, cattle pens, and a big water tower. Today there is nothing left. The first Enterprise school is gone too, abandoned sometime in the late 1930s, and all that remains are memories.

## Happy Memories of Springhouse

For Don Sale of Nanaimo, his years in the Cariboo are also among his happiest memories, especially the years 1936-9 when he taught at the one-room school at Springhouse.

He graduated from normal school at Vancouver in 1932 and filled out 100 applications before landing his first position at 100 Mile in 1934. Arriving at the tiny community, the young teacher was welcomed by trustee Lord Martin Cecil and given an upstairs bedroom in the historic 100 Mile lodge. His salary was a munificent $78 a month, and he paid $25 rent and an extra $5 for laundry.

But, Sale discovered, the school had not yet been built so the bar room in the old partially vacated 100 Mile roadhouse tavern was cleaned up to serve as a classroom. He taught in the bar room until a new one-room school was built the following year in a meadow two miles north of Exeter Station. After two years at the new 100 Mile school, Don moved to Springhouse where he boarded with the George Stafford family.

*Don Sale's first Cariboo classroom was in the old 100 Mile tavern.(center of photo)*

The one-room Springhouse school, built in 1917 from logs felled, limbed, trimmed, and snaked out of the nearby bush, was chinked with a mixture of moss and mud. Heated with a 45-gallon oil drum turned on its side, it devoured cordwood by the arm-load. Usually the oldest boy in the school had to bring in the wood and this job fell to Mike Isnardy, while his sister Alice did the sweeping up after classes. They were paid $5 a month for their chores.

Inkwells froze in winter, and coal-oil Aladdin lamps supplied light on dull days. The students often brought soup, cocoa or milk to school in Rogers Golden Syrup pails and they would be put on the heater to warm for lunch. "We had to ease up the lid a bit," Don remembered, "or sometimes pop! and the lid would fly off."

There were five rows of seven desks, each nailed to 2x4 runners which could easily be moved when sweeping the wood floors with 'Dustbane', or to clear the school for dances, concerts, and church services. "I can remember Jimmy Isnardy and Antone Boitanio on the violins," Don said, smiling. "We would have a rocking good time until dawn."

He can remember each of his pupils too–the six Isnardys, three Johnsons, four Bowes, four Felkers, five Inschos, and one Petrowitz who came by horseback from Chimney Lake, seven miles away.

In those days each school was run by a local school board and at Springhouse the board consisted of Charlie Harris, Edith Stafford, and Marie Sorenson. There were 600 of these small boards throughout B.C. at that time. Repairs, maintenance, and school

*Springhouse School, here in 1926, was twenty years old when Don Sale arrived in the middle of the Depression. He fondly recalls twenty-three students by day and a host of community gatherings. (Ben Clarke photo)*

supplies were all supplied by raising money through box socials, concerts, picnics, and dances. Exercise books, erasers and rulers cost five cents each, pencils two for five cents. Money was scarce and only the bare essentials were bought, often with the teacher footing the bill.

Teachers would only go "out" for Christmas, Easter, and summer holidays. Don recalled how Clarence Stephenson of the IT Stage Line would get on the "howler," the single telephone line from Williams Lake to Dog Creek and announce when his "teachers' stage" would be leaving the lake town for Ashcroft and the CPR.

Coming back, he would meet them at Ashcroft with a cheery "How many for Cariboo?" then it would be off in one of his big seven-passenger touring cars, either a McLaughlin-Buick or Studebaker, finally reaching Williams Lake nine hours later. Clarence was a big man in his 40s at that time, an affable good-hearted person who loved to chat and visit all along the way.

The little Springhouse school was closed in June 1952, and sat empty for twenty years before it was moved and restored as a school "museum" at the Springhouse Trails Guest Ranch. In more recent years it has been renovated as a guest cabin.

I wonder if a small ghost sometimes flits across the floor with a Rogers Syrup Can in hand looking for the old drum heater?

# Columneetza, Meeting Place of the Princely People

Columneetza. It's an Indian word that slides softly over the tongue. Most people are probably unaware it was the original name given to the lake we now know as Williams Lake, and that the San Jose River, which winds its pretty way up from Lac la Hache, was once called the *Rivière de Columneetza*.

To explain the history behind this intriguing name, I should tell you first about the towering rock outcropping known as Signal Point, which can be seen looming over Highway 97 midway down the north shore of Williams Lake.

According to legend, the huge landmark was once the meeting place of Indians of the Athapaskan group. This ancient tribe, a race of proud handsome people, migrated south many eons ago, and penetrated as far as Lytton. Some even managed to make their way to the southern United States and became the forefathers of the Navajos and Apaches.

Williams Lake (as it was later known) was the centre of the district from Lytton to Fort St. James, and it seems likely that it became the meeting place for all the bands of this nation. Thus it is speculated that the bluff was probably used as a signal point in those bygone days; that a warrior could stand on the cliff and from that vantage point signal up and down the lake. This main body of Athapaskans in British Coumbia were later pushed back north in front of the wave of Shuswap people, but not before they had left their mark in naming the local lake and river "Columneetza."

The late Judge Henry Castillou of Williams Lake who was a noted authority on Indian lore and anthropology, deduced that in the Athapaskan language, Columneetza meant "meeting place of the

*Northbound traffic on Highway 97 are welcomed to Williams Lake by clear blue waters on the left and the cliffs of Signal Point, above to their right. (Lakeside Colour Productions Ltd., Williams Lake, BC photo)*

princely people" which certainly ties in with the history of Signal Point. Only a couple of historical references to the name "Columneezta" remain, however. In a small magazine called *The Leisure Hour* printed in 1865 in London, England, an article entitled "To the Cariboo and Back" records the journey of W. Champness and his nameless nephew who travelled from England to the Cariboo diggings at Antler Creek in the year 1862. He writes:

> "William's Lake–also called Columetza [sic] is about forty miles south of Fort Alexander. It is surrounded by some comparatively fertile land, and farming to some extent is carried on. We were truly glad to rest awhile at an inn here. Immediately on our arrival we ordered a 'square meal', and an ample supply of fresh beef, beans, cabbage, pies, milk, tea and coffee was set before us, to which we did justice in a manner which we should have been almost ashamed for our English friends to witness."

The inn which Champness refers to was probably William Pinchbeck's restaurant which he established at the first Williams Lake settlement, now known as the Comer, northwest of the present city.

The only other references I have found to "Columneetza" are on maps cartographed in the 1850s and both Williams Lake and the San Jose River are distinctly marked with the name "Columneetza." I'm not sure when they were changed, but there is no doubt that Columneetza Lake was renamed to honour the first Chief William of the local Indian band who in 1859 was credited with averting war between the whites and native bands when prospectors started pushing up into the Cariboo.

I don't have much information on the San Jose River or why it was changed from Rivière de Columneetza, but according to Margaret Whitehead who wrote an impressive historical book on St. Joseph's Mission near Williams Lake, it was named for Jose (Joseph) Tresierra (see Chapter 6) who in 1859 owned land nearby on Three Mile Creek.

As a young man, Tresierra came north from Mexico searching for gold, but instead became an oxen freighter on the trail from Yale to Barkerville. He is buried at Clinton. Somehow I find it hard to understand why his name would be prefixed with "San" which means "saint" in Spanish.

It seems more likely that the San Jose took its name from the Catholic mission which was established on the little river near 150 Mile House in 1866-7. Called St. Joseph's Mission, it was named for Saint Joseph, the faithful guardian of Jesus and Mary.

But the name "Columneetza" has not disappeared. In 1968 when a handsome new senior secondary school was built at Williams Lake, a contest was held to choose a suitable name. "Columneetza" was submitted by student Gib Scott who remembered the name from an historical article in the *Tribune*, and it was chosen from all the entries, thus preserving for generations to come a little bit of early Williams Lake and Cariboo-Chilcotin history.

The name "Signal Point" will also be remembered. That name was given to a road, now dotted with modern homes, which winds down from the highway and along the lake below the sheer bluff. And on one of those private properties can be found a number of keekwillie holes (pit houses), mute evidence of native habitation of long ago.

# From Bed Springs
## to Billy Goats

She is the only woman to ever take a pack train by herself from Keithley Creek over the mountains to Barkerville, a long lonely haul through miles of wilderness.

But Melva Kinvig was not afraid. "Perhaps a little worried at times," says this pioneer lady who in the 1930s also packed freight regularly to the Midas, Yankee Belle, and Snowshoe mines beyond Yanks Peak high above the timberline.

Although she is now confined to a wheelchair at Deni House in Williams Lake, 87-year-old Melva still vividly recalls those early years when she got up at four in the morning at her home at Keithley Creek, fed and watered the horses, then after breakfast lifted and lashed on the heavy sacks of freight–carrying everything from groceries, coal, and machinery, to six-foot lengths of lumber and once, an unwieldy set of bed springs.

With her string of seven horses, the young wife and mother would be off on the trek to the mines, twelve miles straight up the mountain, picking her way along narrow "game" trails and steep rock bluffs where any misstep could mean a plunge hundreds of feet to the valley below. For the return trip the same day, the horses would be turned loose and would unerringly head home, Melva following. "They knew where the food bucket was," she says, chuckling.

At first Melva accompanied her husband Tom, who initiated her into the rigorous life of packing, and they did lose a horse on one trip. "It stumbled and went over the cliff into the river below, and we lost the whole load and the horse."

Together they packed with their twenty-horse string through blinding snowstorms so bad they could not find their tracks coming back; and through snow so deep "we had to carry an axe to cut the limbs off trees 20 feet up, so the horses could get through without tearing the packs off."

Although only of average height, Melva was well built, vigorous and strong, and soon was packing on her own. She always carried a gun, but only had to use it once when a bear would not get off the trail. "I had to shoot him as the horses were afraid," she says matter-of-factly.

With Tom's instruction, Melva learned to repair her own saddles and equipment, shoe the horses, and even make her own horseshoes—pumping the bellows to get the forge heated, then bending the iron, which was delivered in 100-pound kegs, into the right shape for nailing onto the horses' hooves. Somehow she also coped with bringing up two daughters, tending a house and big garden, and looking after farm animals.

Melva lightly dismisses the dangers and loneliness of those early years of packing into the remote area. "It was a living, a job," she says. "And besides I always loved horses and working with them."

Born in Cherry County, Nebraska in 1910, Melva Morgan was only five when her parents came north by covered wagon to homestead first in Waskenau, Alberta, then in 1927 at Hixon near Quesnel.

Two years later Melva got a job as cook-housekeeper at the Crosina's 153 Mile stopping house where she met stagecoach driver and freighter Tom Kinvig who stopped there regularly. Married in 1931, they went to live at Keithley Creek where Tom, along with two partners—George Woodland and Jack Mackenzie—was building the thirteen-room Keithley Hotel, as well as running a pack train up to the mines operating around Yanks Peak.

Melva, naturally enough, became chief cook and bottlewasher. Those were the days of outside privies and gas lamps, and water had to be hauled in a big drum from nearby Grotto Creek on a horse-drawn stoneboat.

The Kinvigs sold out a few years later and that's when Melva started accompanying her husband on his pack trips to the mines, eventually tackling the lonely mountain trails on her own when Tom was off mining or freighting. When the mines closed at the beginning of World War II, Melva's packing days came to an end, except for that memorable 40-mile trip to Barkerville by herself in the early 1940s.

It was the longest and most challenging haul she had ever tackled. Leaving Keithley with her packtrain, she picked up a load of "schellite," an extremely heavy pale green fluorescent ore used in submarines and found on an outcropping on Snowshoe Mountain. Each small bag weighed 100 lbs. and she loaded two to a horse before heading for the smelter at the historic gold rush town.

In the late 1940s Tom bought the Keithley-Williams Lake mail and freight line, and a couple of years later Melva was on the road again with her husband, making history as the first woman trucker in the Cariboo. "It took about four hours of hard driving to make the 90-mile run to Williams Lake," recalls Melva. The dirt road was so narrow that "if you met in the wintertime, someone had to back up so you could pass."

During spring breakup or rainy weather, it was incredibly awful with deep ruts of slimy black ooze so deep that the Kinvigs usually carried slings of slab wood on the side of their trucks to bridge the worst spots. In the summer they battled dust, washboard, and, as their trucks had no air conditioning then, intense heat.

Around 1953 the couple moved to Williams Lake where Tom took over the Home Oil Bulk plant, but Melva continued to make the mail and freight run to Keithley and back, in fair weather and foul, twice a week.

Her experiences would fill a book. Like the frigid January morning when her one-and-a-half ton truck hit a rock and did an abrupt about face on the ice-packed ruts of Spanish Hill, the steepest part of her 90-mile run, with a drop of 300 to 400 feet to the Cariboo River far below. Fighting the wheel, not daring to touch the brakes, she slithered and bumped her way to the bottom again and admits to being "a little bit shaken up." Melva courageously decided to give the hill another try, and this time made it. "The mail, even if it was only an Eaton's catalogue or a birthday card, meant so much to those lonely trappers, prospectors, and ranchers. I couldn't let them down."

She remembers driving through windstorms so fierce that broken trees were hurled across the windshield; and of stopping to put on chains with wolves howling at her from the tree line. But it could be beautiful too with wildflowers carpeting the hillsides in the spring, deer and moose coming out to feed along the way, and the many creeks and lakes reflecting the deep blue Cariboo sky.

Before each run she made the rounds of the Williams Lake stores, picking up her mail, freight and items for country folk—everything

*Melva Kinvig carried the mail over the rough and rugged 174 mile round-trip haul between Williams Lake and Keithley for a quarter of a century. Until her seventieth year she loaded her stage, took to the road she loved, squeezed by logging trucks when necessary, helped those in need of an emergency lift, scooped rancher's mailbags off their roadside fence, carted outgoing mail from places like Hydraulic and visited her favourite watering station. (Eleaner Howard photos—courtesy Edna Jacobson)*

from hair curlers and wedding gowns, to beer, baby chicks, and billy goats. Nothing was too much trouble for this cheerful courier who made stops and friends all along the way and was rarely late even if she took time to help pick up the telephone line and drape it over the fence posts to improve the reception to Keithley. "One rancher said he could set his clock by me," she says with some pride.

For years she was a familiar and welcome sight as she delivered and picked up mail at the Big Lake, Likely, and Keithley post offices, and ranchers' "way bags" hung on gates along the route. Often she was flagged down by people wanting her to deliver a message: "Ask John if he can bring his bull tomorrow," and on the way back she would report, "John says he will bring the bull."

There were moments of tragedy too. Occasionally Melva would pick up a passenger, if there was no other way for them to get up or down the line, and one day she gave a ride to old Andy Hall, dropping him off at Duck Creek near evening where a trail went into his cabin. She was not allowed to go off the main road, so Andy stacked his parcels and boxes, covered them with a tarpaulin near the road, and said he would get them in the morning.

Coming out from Keithley the next morning, Melva was surprised to see his things still beside the road. Following behind with the big freight truck, husband Tom decided to investigate and a little way in on Andy's trail, found his body.

"He must have died suddenly, seconds after I left him," Melva sadly recalled. She sometimes too brought elderly people in to the Senior Citizens' Home at Williams Lake, those who were too old and feeble to cope with the rugged mountainous existence any more, and remembered how much they hated leaving their wilderness homes in the remote hills of Cariboo.

Melva was a grandmother and still trucking and delivering the mail up until 1969 when they sold the business. Tom, who trapped and worked his mining lease around Little Snowshoe until he was in his eighties, died in 1993.

Melva's life is an incredible story of hard work, courage and resourcefulness, but looking back she says, "I had a wonderful life. I wouldn't have changed a thing."

## Keeping the Peace
## in the Good Old Days

> A considerable stir was created in the jungle at Williams Lake when an Alaskan Indian named Alfred Starr ran amok.
>
> This brought Sgt. Gallagher on the double and in the ensuing battle, three rounds were fought. The Indian, a powerful man, put up a tremendous fight before he was subdued by the policeman.
>
> The battle lasted 20 minutes, with the Sergeant emerging with only a slight injury to his left thumb.

That colourful tale dated July 9, 1931, comes from the *Tribune* files and leads me into my story of Sergeant Frank W. Gallagher who was the first police officer in Williams Lake.

"He was a good man, a good policeman, and a good friend," said the late Ben Clarke who knew Gallagher well. "He was a square shooter." Ben had nothing but praise for the B.C. policeman who kept law and order in Williams Lake for fifteen years. He described him as a man of medium height, spare but well-built.

Sgt. Gallagher rarely wore his uniform, preferring instead to cover his territory in ordinary clothes with just a star over his left breast to indicate his profession. "But he could handle himself," said Ben, who maintained that Gallagher rarely carried a gun and could quell a disturbance by merely keeping the offender "off balance."

Frank Gallagher joined the B.C. Police in 1913 and served at Field, Arrowhead, and Golden before going overseas with the 54th Kootenay Battalion, CEF, a move which led him into an exciting

*Police headquarters were at 150 Mile House when Frank Gallagher rode into town in 1921. (Photo courtesy of Wilf Moore)*

war career. Soon after arriving in England he was placed in the secret service and roved throughout the British Empire on various missions.

After the war, he returned to his police job at Golden, then served at Lucerne, Brittania Beach, and New Westminster before being posted to the 150 Mile House in 1921. Still a busy junction on the Cariboo Wagon Road boasting a school, hotels, bank, stores, government offices, and a jail, 150 Mile House was an old established community whereas the little village of Williams Lake had come into being just two years previous.

But those were boom years for Williams Lake. The town was a beehive of workmen, cowboys, PGE employees, gold seekers heading for the Cedar Creek strikes near Likely, and people from all walks of life eager to establish themselves in the new town. Each new building, no matter how small, was opened with a big celebration and dance. Undoubtedly there was more need of a policeman here than at 150 Mile House, and Sgt. Gallagher became a familiar sight on the road as he went back and forth between the two communities in his two-wheel sulky pulled by a small black horse.

Ben Clarke remembered Gallagher holding court in the old Pinchbeck/Borland house on the Stampede grounds where there was a small jail dating back to the late 1800s when pioneer William Pinchbeck was justice of the peace and maintained law and order in the valley.

In September 1924 Gallagher was given permission to open a police office in Williams Lake, and this was established in the handsome new courthouse built that year on the corner of First and Oliver Street. With two small cells as well as a courtroom, counsel rooms and government offices, it was considered pretty grand at the

*This 1920s perspective of Williams Lake, from the corner of Borland and First, depicts the three symbols of any growing frontier town in the British Empire—a Masonic Hall (left), Bank of Montreal (right), and the new courthouse (background).*

time. I am not sure if Gallagher had any help by then. Even in 1932, records show there were only three B.C. Police officers stationed at Williams Lake and one at Quesnel to police over 100,000 square miles.

As well as quelling disturbances by the use of fisticuffs, Gallagher was often called upon to handle major crimes such as murder and manslaughter, but according to Ben Clarke, he had few enemies.

He was transferred to New Westminster in October 1936, and was killed there not long after in a car accident. Williams Lake and the B.C. Police mourned the loss of a fine policeman and member of the community.

The history of the B.C. Police, the province's first lawmen, goes back to 1858. With the discovery of gold on the Fraser's River, thousands of miners came flooding into the territory and Gov. James Douglas was concerned about keeping law and order in the new colony. Irish-born Chartres Brew was sent out from England to create a "disciplined body of peace officers" and on 19 November, 1858, he became the first commandant of the newly organized force. This B.C. police force enjoyed a proud 92-year history until it was absorbed into the RCMP in August 1950, when the federal force took over law enforcement in unorganized areas and most municipalities in B.C.

Underpaid, overworked, covering vast distances on horseback, and called upon to handle everything from sanitary inspections to

*George McKenzie was a durable hard-working Scot wh*
*policed the Cariboo-Chilcotin in the mid 1920s and after 1930 spent his active and retired life in the Williams Lake vicinity. His accounts were "terse" but he was a very humorous man. (Photo courtesy of B. Poirier)*

rescue operations and murders, they were a remarkable body of men known for their great courage and devotion to duty. In later years when Williams Lake became the headquarters of the great Cariboo district, three men covered an area stretching from Wells/Barkerville down to Clinton and from Anahim Lake in the west to Quesnel Forks in the east.

George McKenzie was one of those dedicated policemen, and his daughter, Barb Poirier of Williams Lake, has kept the little red notebook in which he chronicled his duties every day from June 1923 to April 1926.

George was stationed at Lillooet, but covered a territory that stretched up into the Chilcotin—and he did it on foot, on horseback, by rowboat and occasionally by car, stage or railway. He worked *every* day, month in and month out, Sundays and holidays including Christmas and New Year's Day!

You have to be able to read between the lines of his daily diary to appreciate the amount of work he did. He was the soul of brevity, and his terse little comments fail to reveal the hardships he must have experienced, especially in subzero temperatures.

Here are some examples from 1923:

Dec. 8:   Patrol Sheep Creek and vicinity.
          On foot 15 miles.

Dec. 9:   Patrol Blue Creek and vicinity.
          On foot 15 miles.

Can you imagine slogging along for fifteen miles, probably over snow-covered trails, all in the line of duty, every day? With no separate game branch then, the B.C. Police handled game warden work, hence the many items in George's book to do with patrol and checking of trap lines.

George did occasionally get a little excitement when he had to go to the big city:

April 9:   Lillooet to Vancouver, Oakalla prison with prisoner.
           Train 120 miles, boat 40 miles, auto two miles.

He obviously did not take time to enjoy the bright lights as he returned Friday, faithfully documenting the same number of miles. On Saturday and Sunday, he was back patrolling again, on foot and on horseback.

But the entries that really boggle the mind are dated December 1925 and read:

Dec. 7:   Nemiah Valley to Chilco Lake. Rowboat 28 miles.

Dec. 8:   Marooned on shore at Chilco Lake.

Dec. 9:   To head of Chilco Lake. Rowboat three miles.

Dec. 10:  Head of Chilco Lake, six miles up Ts'il River and
          return Chilco Lake. On foot 12 miles.

Dec. 11:  From head of Chilco Lake to Gold Creek.
          Row boat 22 miles.

Somehow I just couldn't believe George had *rowed* twenty-two miles. Why was he going to Chilco Lake? And why was he marooned? Was the weather bad? Did the rowboat spring a leak? So many questions are left unanswered by his cryptic journal entries.

Since reading George's diary, I have discovered that he was with a party of eleven men sent to investigate a shooting at Chilco Lake. They did indeed row up the lake in two boats which were whipped by four-foot waves, and were marooned there. For more details of this incredible journey, read *Chilcotin-Preserving Pioneer Memories* by the Witte sisters (Heritage House, 1995).

In 1900, B.C. Police Superintendent Hussey said his men "had to have verve, vigour, horse sense, and most important, be of good humour." George certainly had good humour. I remember him in later years as he walked down Oliver Street trailed by his faithful little black Scottie dog. He always had a ready laugh, a twinkle in his eyes, and a quip to make in his rich Scottish brogue. And if you read between the lines of his little red notebook, you find the "verve and vigour" that epitomized a good B.C. policeman. George resigned from the service in 1930, then joined the Indian Department and was posted to Williams Lake as farm instructor and Dominion Constable, a job he held for 21 years.

On 9 November, 1992, Quesnel businessman Lon Godfrey, who served with the B.C. Police in Williams Lake in the late 1940s, presented the city with a handsome plaque commemorating the B.C. Police. It is now part of a permanent collection of old photos and artifacts honouring the force at the Museum of the Cariboo-Chilcotin at Williams Lake.

Those present to reminisce about keeping the peace in the "good old days" were former B.C. policemen Bill Sharpe, Bob Turnbull, Johnny Blatchford, and Ross Goodwin.

A framed honour roll, hand-lettered with the names of all the known policemen who served the Cariboo-Chilcotin since 1860, is part of the display and it includes the names of Bill Broughton who served in the Chilcotin as both policeman and game warden from 1930-42; Tom Hance, first constable in the Chilcotin in 1895, and William Pinchbeck who came to Williams Lake in 1860 and was probably the first constable for the Cariboo.

# Three Longs and a Short

In this age of instant communication, it is hard to believe that telephone operators in Williams Lake were once expected to relay grocery orders, take telegrams, activate the fire alarm, give weather reports, help with crosswords, and of course place phone calls. Incredible as it may seem, one operator was even asked if she knew how to cook a goose.

Even in the 1950s the telephone system was still pretty primitive and I can remember our impatience with it when we first moved up from New Westminster. Yet we couldn't deny a sneaky delight in the cosy neighbourly service, and one of our favourite stories revolves around the time Clive phoned me from Vancouver one evening in 1951.

He placed the call, then patiently waited for it to go through. Finally he could hear the phone ringing, but there was no answer in our apartment over the *Tribune*. Where was I, he wondered? Just then the Williams Lake operator cut in and informed the coast operator that "Mrs. Stangoe is over playing bridge at Mrs. Kerley's. Ask Mr. Stangoe if he would like me to try there?" He did, I was, and the call was completed.

Iris Blair was one of the four operators manning the tiny switchboard at Williams Lake then, tying the community together in a warm personal way that has gone forever.

"Remember how we had to crank a little handle on the side of the box to get the operator?" I asked her as we swapped reminiscences one day. "If you didn't answer, we cranked harder and harder, then wildly, insistently . . . ."

"It didn't do any good," Iris laughed. "There were no lights flashing on and off, just a little 'jack' that dropped down on the first

*Iris Blair handles the telephone switchboard while Claude Barber manages the telegraph inside their Railway Street office in the early 1950s. (Photo courtesy Iris Blair)*

turn." With only one operator handling all the calls from Ashcroft to Quesnel, from Likely to Alexis Creek, it was no wonder that we had to be patient and wait our turn.

Trying to get through a long distance call could be really frustrating. With only one circuit to Vancouver, it sometimes meant a wait of several hours. "People used to accuse us of sleeping on the job," Iris recalled, "but we just had to take it in stride."

There was no telephone directory; we just picked up the phone and asked for our party by name. "Could you get me the Bank of Montreal, Iris?" or "Ring Marguerite Court for me, will you, Iris?" One year the operators typed up a list of telephone numbers in the vague hope that subscribers would use them, but nobody did. There was no strict system for paying your bill every month, either. In fact, ranchers often waited until the fall to settle up after they had sold their cattle.

The operators were the "heart" of Williams Lake, and we all depended on them. Our only physician would notify the telephone office where he would be in case of an emergency, and in the evenings, the two policemen would leave their girlfriends' names.

They even kept track of Homer, the Stangoe's sloppy flop-eared basset hound who roamed the town, phoning to tell us of his

*View of Railway Ave. in the 1920s shows first telephone office (originally telegraph office), far right the Log Cabin Hotel, left, and Fraser & Mackenzie store, centre.*

whereabouts and even taking him into the telephone office on cold miserable days. Then there's the story of the woman who called early one morning and abruptly asked, "What did the princess have?" Puzzled, Iris replied "I beg your pardon?"

The woman again demanded, "What did the princess have?" Then after a pause, she went on, "Well, I know she had a baby, but I don't know whether it was a boy or a girl . . . ." She was referring, of course, to the present Queen Elizabeth and the birth of Prince Charles (November 14, 1948).

In a country where the telephone poles were referred to as "toothpicks" because they were liable to fall down, the operators did their best to ensure that this lifeline was always open. "We tested the lines first thing in the morning," Iris recalled. "I would call Bella Coola first, then Georgina Moon at the top of Sheep Creek Hill and she would answer 'It's a nice day and the lines are clear.' "

The first telephones in the Cariboo made their appearance in 1910 when the federal government installed them in telegraph offices, but they were few and far between. Even by 1937 there were only twenty-four telephones for all of Williams Lake, 150 Mile, and 100 Mile House combined.

But the Chilcotin was worse off. A single line of galvanized wire, mostly strung on trees, was installed from 150 Mile to Bella Coola by 1912. Everyone near the line applied for a phone which was equipped with a horn, or "howler" as it was called, on the wall above it. These units provided great entertainment for the isolated residents who, if they were nearby, could listen to what everyone was saying and get all the gossip back and forth. Not everyone liked it. Incidentally the first telephone in the Chicotin was installed in Becher House, the big popular stopping house at Riske Creek.

It was impossible to phone direct from Bella Coola to Williams Lake, so messages had to be relayed up and down the road. Those travelling the Chilcotin road were often advised, "if you see a line down, hang it back up on a tree."

Pioneer Cariboo telegrapher Hope Patenaude was stationed at Quesnel when the first "howler" type phones were installed in 1910, and years later he recalled, in a *Tribune* interview, the story of the mysterious disappearance of the first phone shipped to Quesnel. Hope had been informed that the new gadget was on its way, but weeks went by and the phone never showed up. The express company managed to trace it to Soda Creek where it had been transferred to a sternwheeler for the trip up river, but from there they drew a blank.

It wasn't until the shipper described the packing box that they got a hint of its whereabouts. The phone had been carefully packed in a government whiskey box, and it was deduced that some artful thief had absconded with it in gleeful anticipation, but when he found only a queer-looking contraption inside, had probably thrown it in the river.

The first (and only) telephone in the new village of Williams Lake for a time was in the Second Avenue home of Chilcotin trucker Tommy Hodgson. His home was a constant hive of activity with people coming and going, looking for messages, wanting to call out, wondering about the road conditions to the Chilcotin, and when the train was due.

The Chilcotin system of "howlers" and telephone wire strung on jack-pines went the way of the dinosaurs when the government replaced the line with the "toothpick" poles in 1942. Japan had attacked Pearl Harbor the previous December and it was thought B.C. might be next, with Bella Coola a likely target. The jack-pine line was woefully inadequate for emergencies.

The first switchboard in Williams Lake was installed in 1941 in the tiny telegraph building beside the Lakeview Hotel and by that time there were 125 telephones in the village. In 1954 when B.C. Tel took over the government-owned system, that number jumped to 340. We still had the crank telephones, mind you.

In 1960 dial service was introduced into Williams Lake and with some regret, we had to accept that the voice asking "number please"

*Trucker Tommy Hodgson installed Williams Lake's first phone in his home on Second Ave. (now Hodgson Mall site) In this photo he is loading a bridge timber on two trucks so it can manoeuver around the hairpin turns of the Sheep Creek hill to the Chilcotin. (BCARS 94628)*

was gone forever. There were still many operators manning the switchboards, however, and in 1971 they made provincial "telephone" history. It is the custom in Williams Lake for everybody to "go western" at stampede time, but the dress code at B.C. Tel prohibited the operators from taking part. This was particularly galling as several were former stampede royalty and had reigned as either queen or princess. So in 1971 the girls refused to go to work unless they too could don cowboy attire for Stampede days. They won their point and as a result were the first operators in B.C. to be allowed to wear jeans on the job.

In the early 1970s BC Tel made local history when the first male operator was hired. His name was Rick Hansen and he went on to bring fame to B.C. and his hometown of Williams Lake for his Man In Motion wheelchair tour around the world.

The last of the old-style phone system was phased out in 1988 with the installation of direct dial phones to Tatla and Puntzi Lake. Prior to that phones in the Central Chilcotin were still on "three longs and a short" (a combination of rings which identified each customer).

The old system was antiquated and aggravating, but it was friendly and human too—like the operators who served us well for so many years.

# The Stagecoach
# Carried a Princess

Princess Margaret has undoubtedly made hundreds of royal visits to far-off places and with time they have probably become blurred in her memory. But I'll bet she has never forgotten her stop in Williams Lake in July 1958 when she was treated to some wild and woolly Cariboo-Chilcotin hospitality.

Those of us who were living here at the time will certainly never forget the sight of the petite Princess careening by in an old BX stagecoach pulled at a dead run by a frightened team of horses.

Unfortunately, many of the 5,000 people who lined the main street were unaware they were witnessing an amazing spectacle, and got only a brief glimpse of the royal visitor as she whizzed by.

Princess Margaret's visit that year was part of the Centennial celebrations throughout the province marking 100 years since the Colony of British Columbia on the mainland had been founded.

This was the first time in the town's history that royalty had visited, so there were great plans to treat her to some of the casual western hospitality for which the town was famous—a luncheon of bacon, eggs, and flapjacks served from a chuckwagon, a chance to see some of the Cariboo's top cowboys in action at the Stampede grounds, and of course the inevitable gift of a Stetson. A stagecoach ride was also suggested several times by local organizers, but always turned down by tour officials.

However, on the night before the big day, Lieutenant-Governor Frank Ross heard of the proposal and asked the Princess if she would be willing to ride in the coach. "I will if you will," she replied bravely.

So, at the last minute, the antique stagecoach owned by Anne and Doug Stevenson was readied for the big event. I have often wondered if the Princess knew she was riding in one of the original B.C. Express stagecoaches used to carry gold, passengers, and mail between Yale and Barkerville in gold rush days. Pockmarked with bullet holes from a long ago skirmish with holdup men, the BX No. 2 was acquired in the early 1920s by Anne's father, pioneer merchant Roderick Mackenzie, not long after he built his general store, the first in Williams Lake, on Railway (Mackenzie) Avenue. Apparently he saw the old relic at Soda Creek, and realizing its historic worth, managed to get the owner to part with it.

He probably never dreamed the old wooden coach would one day become famous again and carry a Princess.

*Princess Margaret's older sister had been Canada's Queen for six years when the princess became Williams Lake's first royal visitor. Here she positions herself in a Cariboo stagecoach and listens attentively to hear what lies ahead.*

On that sunny morning of 18 July, 1958, the sudden change in plans from limousine to stagecoach for the Princess's ride from the Pacific Great Eastern depot to the Stampede grounds caused great consternation. The only team of horses available on such short notice was hitched to a chuckwagon, and there was no time to train them.

Scared by the noise and the crowd milling around the PGE depot, they repeatedly lunged and reared, prompting the Princess to ask "Is it safe?"

But the fun-loving Princess exhibited little nervousness as she was assisted into the historic coach. When Mr. Ross was safely aboard too, the cavalcade with its outriders took off, the terrified team thundering up main street at a full gallop, leaving frustrated security police far behind.

Most of the big crowd lining the street, however, were unaware of the last-minute change and didn't realize the small figure in the pretty lavender dress clutching the open window of the fast-disappearing stagecoach was the Princess.

The coach was finally stopped at the top of the hill above the Stampede grounds because of concerns that the old brakes might fail, and much to her disappointment, the Princess was transferred to a car. She had actually enjoyed the wild ride.

Then, sitting in the chute seats with snorting bulls and ornery broncs right below her, she got a first-hand look at local cowboys as they erupted into the arena. She also enjoyed the "cowboy breakfast" of bacon, eggs, and pancakes so much she asked for a second helping. "My favourite food," she remarked. No kidding.

My husband and I were in the thick of things, of course, rubbing elbows with the big city reporters from London, Hollywood, and

*Mayor Gardner welcoming Princess Margaret at the Williams Lake station. (left to right)  MLA Ray Williston, MLA Bill Speare (background), Lieutenant-Governor Frank Ross, Princess Margaret, Irene and Clive Stangoe, Stampede Queen Jean Stevenson (in cowboy hat), Marie Sharpe (wife of Centennial Chairman Bill Sharpe), Shirley Peterson and her daughter who presented flowers to the Princess, and Mayor Herb Gardner. (*Williams Lake Tribune *photo)*

The antique BX stagecoach had its fifteen minutes of fame when the spunky princess was commandeered for her journey to the Stampede grounds. It was not what officialdom had in mind.

Chicago as well as all the Canadian dailies. Pretty heady stuff for me, a gal who not too long before had been a quiet little housewife in New Westminster. I was close enough to the Princess at the PGE depot to almost end up in the receiving line, and at the Stampede grounds managed to wriggle right up to the royal enclosure where I watched her relax completely, quietly slip off her shoes and lean forward on the top rail to get a closer view of the rodeo events.

I was also fortunate that day to meet two pioneer ladies—Mrs. Agnes (Norman) Lee, 86, of Hanceville and Mrs. Anne (Wayne) Huston, 85, of Soda Creek who were presented to the Princess during the ceremonies at the depot. Later at the Stampede grounds when the official party was served gin and tonics, the Princess's favourite drink, the two ladies passed their glasses over the barricade to me. As visiting newsmen drooled enviously in the summer heat, I sent one over their heads to husband Clive who was covering the scene from a different vantage point. A memorable moment indeed . . . .

Before she left, the Princess presented colourful pioneer Antone Boitanio with the engraved buckle and leather belt he had won at the Stampede that year, for placing first in the old timers' calf roping contest.

Then the Princess was gone, driven to the airport in a sedate limousine, and the stagecoach was retired once more, to be stored again on the Stevenson property on north Lakeside. Several years ago, when the property was sold, the stagecoach was moved to the Kamloops home of Rhona Armes, one of Rod's three granddaughters.

The Museum of the Cariboo-Chicotin at Williams Lake is hoping, however, to be able to purchase the historic coach with the help of a provincial government grant and local donations.

It will then be brought back home to Williams Lake where it will be restored to its former glory and we can remember again its last great ride in the Cariboo when it carried a Princess.

# Freedom Road

It was termed "Bella Coola's wedding day with the rest of British Columbia."

On 26 September, 1953, two catskinners—Alf Bracewell working from Anahim Lake, and George Dalshaug from Bella Coola—pushed aside the last mound of boulders and touched blades high on a mountainside in the Coast Range. Then the two men stepped down and shook hands.

That memorable day marked the completion of the "Freedom Road," the third outlet to the Pacific. Today it is known as Highway 20.

*In the early days men like Lester Dorsey led pack trains over the Precipice Trail, the only route inland from Bella Coola.*

Up until 1953, the only way over the forbidding Coast Range from Bella Coola was a pack horse trail which wound through dense forests and up precipitous slopes to the village of Anahim Lake where the dirt road crossing the Chilcotin plateau from Williams Lake ended. Repeated pleas to the government to complete the link resulted in the answer that it was "impractical." So the determined residents of Bella Coola, sparked by a pioneering Board of Trade headed by fiery Cliff Kopas, embarked on their own plan to "beat the hill" and end their isolation from the rest of the country.

They launched the project in 1951 with $250 and a prayer, and from then on it was two years of backbreaking work. First of all Elijah Gurr slogged hundreds of miles searching for the best route through the unforgiving country; then behind came the workers drilling and blasting sheer rock faces and teetering on the edge of deep canyons, hacking and clearing trees and underbrush.

Impressed with their resourcefulness, new highways minister Phil Gaglardi got the government to kick in with some money from time to time, but mostly it was the people of Bella Coola who were responsible for the planning, the surveying, the building and the financing of the incredible task. Later Gaglardi would term it "magnificent in its conception and outstanding in its completion."

Although the new road was just a narrow torturous trail clinging to cliffs with barely enough room for a single vehicle, it was enough

*Bulldozers meet to complete road to Bella Coola, 26 September, 1953. (Cliff Kopas photo)*

to convince the government that the route was indeed practical. The Department of Highways then took it over and started upgrading the historic link.

The official opening of the road (or the two ruts which passed for a road) took place on 17 July, 1955, at the historic spot on the mountain where the two cats touched blades.

Gaglardi flew into Nimpo Lake, then toughed it out by car to be there for the ribbon cutting and unveiling of the bronze plaque inscribed as follows:

At this site on September 26, 1953
two bulldozers operated by Alf Bracewell and George Dalshaug
touched blades to symbolize
the opening of a road through the mountain barrier of the
coast range marked out by Elijah Gurr.
Two years of strenuous local effort thus established
a third highway route across this province
to the Pacific Ocean through an area originally explored
by Lieut. H. Spencer Palmer, R.E. 1862

Unfortunately the plaque was stolen in later years and has never been recovered.

*Today the Bella Coola hill is still a driving experience. After the road opened even the brave drove it heart-in-mouth.*

A great convoy of people from all over the Cariboo and Bella Coola, plus government officials, converged for the ceremony and as *Tribune* publisher, my husband Clive went along to cover the big event. "It was a trip to end all trips," he wrote. It took more than ten hours to make the ninety miles from Anahim to the port of Bella Coola, and many in the convoy thought the road should promptly be closed again.

Even Gaglardi was overheard to admit that "it was perhaps a bit premature."

As vehicles plunged over the bush road that had been bulldozed through jack-pines, mufflers were ripped off cars, several had to tie up their gas tanks with baling wire, and all were paint scratched and had low-hanging skirts creased. Deputy Minister Evan Jones, riding in his expensive Buick, was not amused. A cloudburst the night before didn't help, and many vehicles bogged down in mud holes half a city block in length. As each car or truck lurched through to the end, the driver was given a resounding cheer.

Clive, however, was impressed with the tremendous accomplishment and wrote: "Looking at the mountain rising to sheer heights above you and down 2,000 feet where Young Creek is lost from view in the depths of the pass, you feel an overwhelming respect for those men who pushed their machines along the side of the mountain, and for the men who before them walked through to find the route and mark it."

The Freedom Road has improved tremendously since then, of course, but many people will remember when large vehicles had to back up to make the sharp hairpin turns; and of creeping down the narrow track which literally clung to the precipices, hoping not to meet anyone coming up. Then there are the tales of those white-faced tourists who flew home rather than face going back up the "infamous" hill or shipped their cars and themselves out by steamship.

It was an awesome project and worth remembering now some forty-odd years later.

# Only in the Cariboo, You Say?

## Ghosts in the Graveyard

Was it murder?

It was midnight and the town was quiet. The little group of men gathered silently in the Williams Lake cemetery, and hoped no one would see them.

Down in a grave, B.C. policeman Bob Turnbull was busy digging up a coffin while Sgt. McClinton hovered above him along with undertaker Alex Clark, coroner Rene Hance, and Dr. Larry Avery who waited with scalpel in hand.

Suddenly a car pulled into the cemetery gate off Comer Street and stopped. The young couple inside, unaware of the eerie goings on, were undoubtedly planning to get cozy and, after all, what better place to smooch than the secluded deserted graveyard on the outskirts of town?

The exhuming party stood motionless, hardly breathing, hoping the lovers would soon leave. The Sergeant, concerned that the nocturnal exhuming would be discovered, whispered to Clark to send the lovebirds on their way. "Tell them we're digging a grave for the morning," added Turnbull. Moments later there was a shower of gravel as the terrified driver abruptly squealed away. Had the shadowy figure of the old coroner, stooped with age, shuffling towards their car, convinced the couple they were seeing a genuine ghost? No one knows.

This happened in the late 1940s after a highly respected rancher died and was brought into Williams Lake for burial. Some weeks after the funeral, a rumour started that he had not died from natural causes, but in fact had been poisoned, perhaps by a family member.

*The 92-year saga of the B.C. Provincial Police was nearing its end in 1949 when this group got together. No doubt a few yarns were spun that day. (Back row l-r) Lon Godfrey, A. Fairburn, NCO I/C; Bob Turnbull (Alexis Creek), Bob Kyte, radio operator. (Front) Leo Jobin, game warden; E. Rosberg, Const. I/C; Rene Hance, coroner, Alexis Creek.*

When the police checked, they found no postmortem had been done and were subsequently instructed by the attorney-general at Victoria to exhume the body and do an autopsy. Rather than arouse suspicion if indeed there was no crime, the local police decided to do the autopsy secretly so the next-of-kin and general public would be unaware of the goings on.

"I thought they were out of their minds," said Dr. Avery when he later recalled his disbelief in being asked to do a graveside autopsy by flashlight in the middle of the night! So on the designated night, the group of men huddled around the open grave as Const. Turnbull finished his digging and unearthed the coffin.

Was it murder? No, the poor old guy had actually died from a perforated duodenal ulcer, a very painful way to go. So the body was carefully returned to the grave, the plot smoothed over and flowers replaced with only two scared lovers and a handful of people in the little village of Williams Lake being any the wiser.

## The Corpse that Didn't Fit

Former B.C. policeman Lon Godfrey has an inexhaustible supply of funny police stories and this is one of them as written by my editor/ husband Clive:

A call came into the police desk at Williams Lake one cold winter night from a resident out Spokin Lake way. The caller was sure something was wrong with a bachelor neighbour as he hadn't seen him for days and there was no sign of life around his cabin.

Lon and fellow constable "Stevie" Stevens agreed to investigate and after a long chilly ride located the cabin and entered it to find the bachelor's body on the bed. But it wasn't just slumped peacefully in the repose of death. One leg jutted out almost at a right angle to the torso, and the opposite arm was flung out in the same manner. Four or five days of 40-below weather had left the appendages frozen stiff in their pose, totally adverse to being rearranged.

The constables faced the problem of fitting the body into their police car. First they tried thawing out the corpse by lighting the cabin heater, but it was soon obvious that it would take a day or so of stoking to achieve any results. They next turned to the improbable task of getting the body through the car door, but all the twisting and pushing was in vain. The car trunk seemed to be the only possibility, and they managed to get the torso and the outstretched arms under cover, but one leg was still out in the elements. It would have to do, they decided, so they tied the trunk lid down and took off for town.

Their strange cargo did not pass unnoticed. They were well on their way when Staff-Sergeant Andy Fairbairn in Williams Lake received an agitated call from Lil Crosina at the 153 Mile Store. "A big black car just went by with a leg sticking out of the trunk!" she reported breathlessly.

In the meantime the two harassed constables drove to the town's chapel/morgue, a small frame building near the old War Memorial Hospital. They managed to get the corpse through the wide doors, but there was no way they could get the body into the empty coffin left there for such emergencies.

The next move was to phone a local doctor who lived nearby. Apprised of the problem, he was soon on the scene equipped with a saw. A few cuts and the problem was solved. The body now fit the coffin.

So help me, Lon says it is true.

## Sailing Cariboo Style

Nothing, but nothing, not even a jail sentence, could stand in the way of sailing on Williams Lake back in the good old days.

Pioneer merchants Roderick Mackenzie and John Smedley started the Williams Lake Sailing Club in the 1920s and had a wonderful time competing against one another. "There's Smedley getting all the wind," Rod would fume as his friend and arch-rival would scud by him in his sailboat, *Saucy Sal*. Then Rod would jibe his own boat, *Anne*, so vigorously that it would often tip over and he would end up in the lake.

There's a delightful account in the *Williams Lake Times*, the village's first newspaper, of a sailing club picnic in 1929. "There was just enough breeze to gently skim over the lake, and the day started with a club cruise with several daintily-trimmed yachts taking part. This ended at 12 noon promptly and a few moments later the good ladies invited all to a most sumptuous repast. Throughout the afternoon the skippers were most generous and load after load of visitors were treated to a sail."

In the winter some of the more rabid enthusiasts would put their sails on ice boats to skim across the lake, or determinedly bump through snow and drifts, all in the interest of good outdoor fun.

*Ice Boats on Williams Lake, 1920s. (Laura Monon photo)*

But it was the annual summer regatta and the thrill of racing to win which created the most interest. And that brings me around to the story of the American sailor who was visiting in the Cariboo one summer and planned on competing in the forthcoming races. Excitement ran high at the thought of this new challenge, and local sailors could hardly wait for the big moment to arrive. But unfortunately just a few hours before the races were scheduled to start, the young man ran afoul of the law (a minor offence, it was said) and was clapped into jail.

Well, there was great consternation throughout the little village at this disruption of the sailing event of the year and something obviously had to be done.

And it was. Somehow the police were persuaded to release the prisoner long enough for him to compete in the races; then he was whisked back to his cell to await Cariboo justice.

There is no report on how the visitor made out, either on the lake or in court, but he must have left believing that the Cariboo-Chilcotin was indeed a wonderful place, full of eccentric people and an accommodating police force.

# Scottish-Indian Pipers from the Cariboo

Most people react with astonishment when they first hear of the unique pipe band from the Cariboo Indian Residential School at St. Joseph's Mission which brought fame to Williams Lake back in the 1960s.

As far as I know, they were the only all-native girls' pipe band in Canada, probably the world. It was a sight never to be forgotten. The young native girls dressed in Scottish kilts enthusiastically skirling the tunes of the Highlands were so good and so unusual that they competed and won against male pipers, toured Canada, appeared on national television, and performed live at Expo 67 in Montreal.

The unlikely premise of training the young girl students to play the bagpipes originated in 1958 with Jim Duthie, a Williams Lake chiropractor who was a piper of some distinction himself. Jim had already formed the 610 (Cariboo) Air Cadet Squadron for native lads at the school when he was asked to organize some recreational activity for the girls, and he came up with the idea of a band to march along with the boys.

Most of us think of the bagpipes as a difficult instrument to master, but according to Margaret (Dick) Gilbert who was with the band from its very beginnings in 1958, it came quite easily. "We learned to read the notes and in no time we were playing a tune," she says. Oddly enough the girls appeared to have an "ear" for the plaintive but stirring music and could even pick up difficult competition tunes just by listening.

"The hardest part was filling out and keeping the bag full and at an even drone," she smiled. "There was a lot of screeching and wailing at first, and the boys teased us. We were so embarrassed." But the

*Little did Margaret (Dick) Gilbert and Elsie Meyers know the fame that lay ahead for the Cariboo Indian Girls Pipe Band when they posed for this photo in their "air force" tartans. (Margaret Gilbert photo)*

girls kept at it and practised faithfully. They also found time to make their own kilts and shawls from a gray-blue "air force" tartan chosen by former RCAF officer Duthie. "One of the nuns who was a seamstress instructed us," recalled Margaret who says it took eight yards for the kilt alone.

Soon the young pipers were appearing at Stampede parades and other local events, and as word of their charm and musical ability spread, they were invited to perform in other communities throughout the province. As they marched along, their tartan skirts swinging, their faces beaming as they puffed and blew on a musical instrument that was so foreign to their culture, they were an instant hit wherever they went.

Then unfortunately Jim moved away. In March 1960 the *Tribune* wondered, "What will happen to the band now that the teacher has gone?" and appealed for another piper to come forward.

Two appeared. Adam Smith and Jimmy Forbes of Quesnel took on the job of training the girls with Adam teaching them the Highland Fling and other Scottish dances while Jimmy concentrated on the drums and pipes. This meant they had to be driven up to Quesnel twice a month on weekends to practice.

"Mr. Smith was a wonderful old man," says Margaret. "I can still see him dancing across the floor, the money jingling in his pockets, saying 'this is the way it goes, lassies' in his rich Scottish brogue." When Adam died in 1964, the entire band played at his funeral. As they performed the haunting "Amazing Grace" at the graveside, the girls started crying, the tears trickling down into their

*In 1960, to keep the band alive, the school bus travelled to Quesnel twice a month where Jim Forbes gave them lessons. (Margaret Gilbert photo)*

mouthpieces, forcing them one by one, to stop playing. Finally there was only one lone piper, Verna Jim, left to play the final bars, the melancholy sound from her bagpipes swirling up in a touching farewell to their beloved instructor.

By now the girls were able to practise right at the school. Cyril Aucoin, who Margaret says "maintained the standards and made everybody learn their notes," was hired as their teacher, and he was followed by Garnet Snow, another excellent piper. Their last instructor was Ramsay Parker, an accountant at the Royal Bank in Williams Lake, who later married Phyllis Bob, a former band member.

In the meantime their fame continued to spread. At the 1964 Calgary Stampede they won first prize for the best Junior Band; at Saskatoon Pioneer Days they bested the men pipers and were also judged the best band in the parade; and, in Winnipeg they performed along with the RCMP M-sical Ride. Their popularity culminated in their participation in the 1965 Dominion Day celebrations on Parliament Hill in Ottawa which were televised to the whole country. It was an exciting and memorable moment for both the girls and those back home in the Cariboo.

Then it was off on a two-week tour of Ontario and Quebec before heading for Nova Scotia where they competed in the Antigonish Highland Games which are the largest highland games in Canada. "It was a wonderful experience to march and play with 600 other pipers," says Margaret as she tried to convey the magnificence of the spectacle.

After that, they continued on to New Brunswick and then ended up with a tour of Prince Edward Island. Everywhere they went, they

They won the hearts of a nation, played from coast to coast and provided life-long memories for both the players and those who heard them (K. Buchanan photo)

attracted huge crowds, and fielded some strange questions. "Some people didn't know we were native; they thought we were just beautifully tanned," smiles Margaret. "Others wanted to know whether we lived in teepees in the winter, and if we spoke English." Another big event for the Indian Girls' Pipe Band was their invitation to appear at Expo 67 in Montreal. Again they drew tremendous crowds as they performed outside the Native Indian pavilion and in the big Expo stadium, and again Cariboo residents basked in their moment of glory.

Coming home through the States, they ran out of funds and had to stop at numerous cities and towns to stage concerts. But this was nothing new for the band who were used to playing at hockey games and other events back home to raise money. The band got some assistance from the Department of Indian Affairs, but Williams Lake business people also gave generously. "Otherwise the band would have disintegrated," says Margaret.

Over the years the girls danced and played their way into the hearts of people throughout British Columbia and across Canada. As they grew up and left school, younger ones took their place, but always the same high standards continued. Incidentally, Duthie started with 16 students; by 1966 the band numbered 23, ranging in age from 11 to 18 years.

"It (playing in the band) was the most positive part of my life," Margaret says. "It kept me going and gave me the courage do something with my life. Our instructors were a real inspiration and instilled in us that we were as good as anyone else."

Margaret was with the band for six years, latterly as pipemajor, then went on to become a self-employed human services counsellor. She flies all over Canada as well as Alaska and the United States— wherever she is needed, she says, "to heal the wounds of the past." Some of the other young pipers have found success too, as teachers, nurses, lawyers, and chiefs of their bands.

I'm not sure just when the band was disbanded. Margaret says it just "faded away." However in 1971 due to the integration of native children into district schools and the opening of more day schools on reserves, the Cariboo Indian Residential School was closed. This undoubtedly spelled "finish" to the band.

But those of us who were fortunate enough to see and hear the marvellous Scottish-Indian pipers from the Cariboo-Chilcotin will never forget them.

# The Bridge that Rudy Built

The story of how Cariboo rancher Rudy Johnson built his own private bridge across the mighty Fraser River defies the imagination.

His remarkable achievement began, oddly enough, with his wife's near fatal accident at the Soda Creek ferry one day in the spring of 1965. Helen was on her way home with supplies for their Buckskin Ranch about eight miles below Soda Creek on the west side of the river. The river was running high but the little open cable ferry which held only two cars made the trip safely.

Rufus Wilson, the ferryman, wasn't feeling too well that day, and when Helen kindly went to help him tie up at the far shore, she slipped on the wet decking and plunged into the brown roiling water. She couldn't swim. As the current threatened to sweep her down river, she made a convulsive grab for a log which had jammed under the ferry slip and managed to climb out.

Rudy was pretty upset. "That's when I decided to put a bridge across," he says, then adds with a chuckle, "I also bought my wife a bathing suit."

Except for the tiny ferry, which could not handle big logging or cattle trucks, the only way out from their ranch to Williams Lake was by way of a rough dirt road through Meldrum Creek to Highway 20, which in winter or wet weather became an almost impassable morass of deep greasy Cariboo mud. Altogether, after crossing the Fraser at the Chilcotin/Chimney Creek bridge, it was a trip of forty-eight miles into town.

Rudy spent days studying the river, upstream and downstream, flying in his own plane over the canyon to pick out the best route for a bridge and walking along the shoreline studying water levels and

*The old Soda Creek ferry, now gone, and the ferry slip in foreground, where Helen Johnson almost lost her life. (*Williams Lake Tribune *photo)*

types of rock. Finally he was ready with his drawings. "A lot of people thought I was crazy," Rudy observed, "but once I had the idea, I knew it could be done." After all, when just a kid of fourteen he had used a high rigger to bring up a locomotive from the depths of Cowichan Lake on Vancouver Island.

The next step was to tackle Highways Minister Phil Gaglardi for help with his mammoth project, but although Gaglardi thought it

*When Rudy Johnson pointed to the far shore of the Fraser River in 1967*
*and said "That's where the bridge is going," few believed he could make*
*it happen. (Photo courtesy Rudy Johnson)*

was a "hell of a good idea," he could not help the determined rancher
financially.

He did suggest, however, that Rudy show his sketches to a
Vancouver engineer to see if the plan was feasible. But the elderly
engineer rejected the idea as impossible and commented with some
amusement, "When did you have your last medical, young fellow?"
But Rudy had always been a man who met challenges head on and
that is when he decided to quit talking and "just do it."

A pilot friend had spotted an abandoned bridge in Alaska near
Moose Pass on the Kenai River. Left high and dry when an earthquake
had changed the course of the river, it could not be used elsewhere
as Alaskan road standards had changed and it was now six inches
too narrow.

Rudy bought it for $40,000 and in February 1968 flew up with
three men, and proceeded to take it apart, numbering the pieces as
they went, then loading the 3,000 bridge parts onto four railroad

cars. Taken by low-bed trucks to the saltchuck, thirty miles away, then by barge to Prince Rupert, the cars rolled via the CN Railway to Prince George, then by Pacific Great Eastern (B.C. Rail) to Williams Lake. There they were shifted to trucks again for the final run to the selected site on the west side of the river.

In the meantime, Rudy had also been busy getting financing for his dream of spanning the turbulent Fraser. Five coastal and nine Cariboo investors had faith in Rudy's ability and a company called, appropriately enough, Fraser River Crossing Ventures Ltd., was formed. He also hired Victoria engineer Howard Elder who, intrigued with the bold scheme, agreed to be his project manager. Now came the biggest challenge of all for the 45-year-old rancher: putting the 200-ton bridge together and getting it across the river.

First of all, access roads had to be carved and blasted out of the steep rock bluffs leading down to the canyon on both sides, and cement abutments made. The east side was relatively easy; the cement was brought the ten miles up the old Soda Creek highway from Williams Lake by Cariboo Redi-Mix, but the west side had to be done by hand with a tractor and cement mixer.

"We worked night and day nonstop for three days," recalled Rudy. His five-man crew consisted of himself, his two sons Bob and Randy, and Martin Stacey and son Ian, augmented from time to time with a couple of men from the nearby Soda Creek Reserve. Then came the task of putting those 3,000 pieces together on the Buckskin Ranch road, picking up the reassembled 300-foot steel bridge, and swinging it over the river with two big skylines (cables) anchored to the ground.

Sounds simple, but it was an unbelievable feat for such a small crew working against almost overwhelming odds. Incredibly, by the fall of 1968, the job was done. The total cost: around $200,000, with no help from any level of government.

Although news of Rudy's remarkable do-it-yourself bridge was brought up in the House of Commons by Cariboo-Chilcotin MP Paul St. Pierre, and the Hon. Arthur Laing, Minister of Public Works, had indicated on national television that he would attend the official opening, nothing happened.

There was no fanfare, no ribbon cutting, no speeches. In late November two cattle trucks owned by Elton Elliott and driven by Ken Boychuk and Jim Pigeon rumbled across the new bridge. They were the first commercial vehicles over the span. The bridge was open.

*Rudy Johnson's bridge still stands as a Cariboo monument to sheer determination and know-how in an age when red tape could not smother pioneer initiative. (Lakeside Colour Productions photo)*

"I've never regretted doing it," says Rudy who maintains that it could not be done today. "Too much red tape and bureaucracy; they would stop you before you got out of your truck." In 1967 he didn't even need to get a permit, believe it or not, as the Fraser was not a navigable river at that particular point.

To offset their costs, Rudy and his associates had to charge tolls for commercial trucks using the new bridge, but drivers were happy to pay as no longer did they have to go the long way around via Meldrum Creek. Private vehicles were free.

So it remained, the only privately owned toll bridge on the North American continent until it was purchased in 1978 by the provincial government and became part of the massive highways system of British Columbia. (Could there have been some red faces in Victoria?)

It is still known as Rudy Johnson's Bridge, a testimonial to one man's daring and courage.

But those who have known Rudy a long time were probably not surprised that he could pull off such an amazing feat. After all, the life story of this modern day pioneer, a man with little formal education, is peppered with the impossibles. He was born in northern Sweden above the Arctic Circle. His engineer father, Axel, came to Canada in the early 1900s to work on the CN Railway, later the PGE, before settling down on a farm at Aldergrove with his family in 1931.

But son Rudy hated farming and at a young age struck out on his own, working in logging camps on the coast until 1947 when, impressed by the massive timber stands in the Cariboo, he established a sawmill in a remote area on the west side of the Fraser near Soda Creek, then another at 153 Mile.

There was little the young entrepreneur would not try. In 1954 he punched the first forestry "fire" road through from Horsefly Lake to Quesnel Lake, battling for twenty-eight miles through swamp, trees, and stumps with just a small caterpillar. He constructed, remodelled and moved buildings in and around Williams Lake, learned to fly and established Chilcotin Airways along with Fred Bass, Bert Lloyd, and Bert Goodrich as a prospecting venture.

When Lloyd and Goodrich went missing on a flight out of Vanderhoof in 1956, Rudy flew countless miles over the rugged countryside searching for the two young men. They were not found for sixteen years. Their plane, overloaded with mineral samples, had gone down in a small deep lake north of Fort St. James, but it was not until 1972 that extremely low water levels revealed the wreck.

When a big radar station was established at Puntzi Mountain in the Chilcotin in 1953, Rudy was there building the roads and runways, then it was away to work on the La Joie Dam on Bridge River.

He was also a partner in Central Aircraft Salvage and Leasing in Vancouver (now Con-Air) which was involved in salvaging airplanes all over the world. When a PWA Beaver crashed into remote Lorna Lake near Big Creek in the Chilcotin in October 1960, killing the pilot and three geologists, Rudy arranged for the wreck to be brought up from the depths, then with the help of Dick Church and Marcel Marcotte winched it onto a sled made of spruce logs, and dragged it by cat through the mountains. It took two weeks in incredibly awful 20-below weather, but the plane was eventually reconstructed, and still flies out of Campbell River.

In 1961 he bought the Buckskin Ranch (so called for a native nicknamed "Buckskin" because he got so many skins while trapping) and over the next twenty-eight years raised cattle, logged, and enlarged and improved the operation.

Selling in 1989 to the D. F. Hoffmeister family, he is now retired, more or less, and lives on the north lakeside in Williams Lake where he can look across the lake to the small subdivision he is developing on a hillside off the Dog Creek road, and can fume about the many restrictions today.

Building a bridge across the Fraser in 1968 was no big deal.

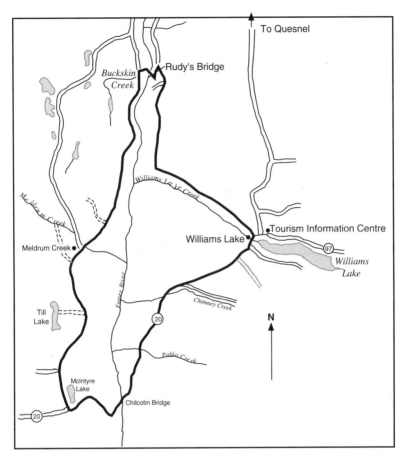

*Map showing long route through Meldrum Creek to Williams Lake over Chilcotin bridge, as compared to crossing on Rudy's bridge and travelling the old Soda Creek road south to town.*

# Three Against the Wilderness
# Homesite Restored

Like many others in the Cariboo-Chilcotin, I was a mite upset a few years ago when I heard that the original Meldrum Creek homesite made famous by Eric Collier in his international best seller, *Three Against the Wilderness*, might be destroyed.

The buildings, owned by the Department of National Defense, are located on the Chilcotin Military Reserve north of Riske Creek, and in 1989 it was contended that the land was needed for army manoeuvers and the deteriorating structures would have to be demolished or moved.

The original cabin where Eric, his wife Lillian, and son Veasy first lived had already collapsed with time and weather, but their second four-room log home built in 1946, as well as a hunter's cabin and log barn, were still standing, although the roofs were caving in and they too were in danger of succumbing to the elements.

When the story about the possible destruction of the homesite appeared in the *Williams Lake Tribune*, there was great consternation among local heritage buffs, but no one seemed to be able to come up with the money or a solution of how to preserve the derelict buildings.

Then with a change of heart in the summer of 1994, the word came that the buildings could stay on the Army Reserve, and not only that but the Chilliwack-based Canadian Army Engineers, headed by Capt. Paul Davies who was aware of the historic significance of the homesite, went to work and completely restored the Collier home, cabin and log barn, giving them a new lease on life. All three were reroofed and finished with shakes, and new doors and windows installed, helped by donations of material from Williams Lake firms. The army also built a bridge and improved the roads into the meadow.

In September that year, on a glorious autumn day with a warm sun etching golden poplars against a vivid blue Chilcotin sky, I made my first trip out to see the historic site. In my innocence I had originally thought I could drive out in my car, hang a right at Riske Creek and drive along until I came to the homesite. Fortunately friend David Bateson took me in his pickup truck, otherwise I never would have made it.

You definitely need a guide. Once off Highway 20 the roads skittered off in all directions, and I was lost. But David knew which one led to the homesite and I then discovered why we needed a truck. Pot-holed, rutted, "corduroyed" in spots with small logs, the road meandered for forty kilometers up and down dale, through trees and small bogs. We were over an hour reaching the homesite, and I tried to imagine what it must have been like in the 1930s when it took the Colliers eight hours to go in by team and wagon.

Finally David and I arrived at the grassy flat where the Colliers lived in isolation for twenty-seven years and endured many frightening experiences in their fight for survival.

The abandoned homesite was eerily quiet, and I almost felt like tiptoeing as we wandered around taking photographs, then walked over to stare with disbelief at the massive 300-foot dam Eric and Lillian had erected across Meldrum Creek using just shovels and wheelbarrows in their efforts to bring water and wildlife back to the arid terrain. In all, they hand-built thirty dams.

I tried to imagine Eric writing his book in the little log house at night, after he had spent a long day hunting, working the trap line, and coping with the hardships of his primitive surroundings.

"He loved to write," says son Veasy of Williams Lake who recalled how his father first started writing articles for the *Northwest Digest* at Quesnel, then in 1949 for *Outdoor Life* becoming the first nonresident to win the U.S. magazine's coveted Conservation Award. At the urging of publishers, he began to think about a book and by 1955 had completed seven chapters of *Three Against the Wilderness*. During the winter of 1957-8 he wrote another twenty-three to finish his epic story. Published in 1959, it has been translated into seven languages, condensed for *Reader's Digest*, and reprinted many times.

"He wrote by longhand," says Veasy. "He would sit in his favourite armchair, place a piece of plywood across the arms, then write for hours by lamp light." Later he would tap out his manuscript on an old Remington typewriter.

*In 1942 tents were still a part of daily life as Eric heads out to Riske Creek in need of supplies. In 1959 Eric Collier is seen here next to the "hunter's cabin" and a substantial wolf pelt. (Photo courtesy Veasy Collier)*

Eric Collier was born in 1903 in Northhampton, England, the son of a successful iron foundry owner. He was just fourteen when he joined the navy and served two years as a signalman. Returning home, he knew he didn't want to go into business, so his father sent him out in 1920 as a "mud pup" to his cousin, Harry Marriott (author of *Cariboo Cowboy*) who was homesteading near Clinton. ("Mud pup" was the common term given to young Englishmen whose families in those days sent them out to learn ranching in Canada. They usually got the more menial chores of shovelling manure, building fences, and looking for strays.)

The tall lanky Englishman fell in love with the Cariboo-Chilcotin while working for Marriott, then at the Gang Ranch, Cotton Ranch, and for Fred Becher at his popular stopping house near Riske Creek. This is where in 1928 he married Lillian Ross, a petite young local girl who, despite a hip deformity caused by a childhood accident, cheerfully started out three years later on the torturous trail to the Meldrum Creek area with her husband, 18-month old son Veasy, three horses, a wagon, a tent, a heavy load of provisions, and $33 in cash, all their worldly possessions.

At first the family lived in an abandoned little log home built by "Trapper" Tom Evans, a master carpenter who also built the big Cotton ranch house and the second Becher stopping house in 1915. This log cabin was in Stack Valley, ten miles from where Eric wanted to develop his "dream" at Meldrum Creek, a long way to travel every day by team and wagon or on horseback. So a few years later the Colliers moved to the home site, existing at first in the tent until they could build their first small cabin.

Although the family accepted the loneliness and isolation as a way of life, they were still keenly interested in the outside world and Veasy can remember his dad selling his favourite saddle horse in 1939 so he could buy a radio and keep up on the news of World War II.

Eric eked out a living by trapping, hunting, and big game guiding. His guide's licence was the second one to be issued in the Chilcotin. Along with Ed Bob, he organized the B.C. Registered Trappers Association in 1946, and became its first president. He attended many game conventions and that is where he honed his skills as a formidable speaker. He never backed down in an argument, particularly in his disputes with the B.C. Game Department over their game management policies. Nevertheless he was always highly respected for his views.

*Eric's chair and Lillian's chair. Many an evening while Eric sat here reading or writing his famous story, Lillian focussed on her crocheting. (Photos courtesy Veasy Collier)*

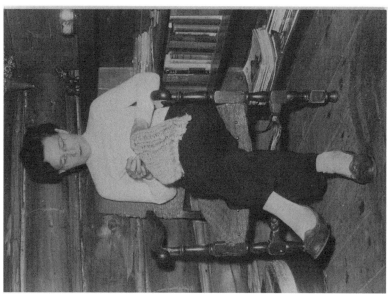

But above all he was an ardent outdoorsman, a naturalist who was described in a *Tribune* article as a "woodsman who strolled through the forest as if he were part of it. Gun crooked comfortably under his right arm, he strode along the top of a beaver dam as if it were Park Avenue."

Working in conjunction with the Society for the Prevention of Cruelty to Animals in the mid 1950s, Eric did field tests on a prototype of the Conibear trap (invented by Frank Conibear) and following a two-part article in *Outdoor Life* in which he recommended the more humane device, the trap went into production and is still widely used today.

After Clive and I took over the *Tribune* in 1950, Eric often dropped in, usually with an article or letter to the editor expounding his favourite subject—conservation—and we soon came to know and like this unassuming quiet-spoken man. We had no idea he would one day write a book that would become a classic of wilderness writing.

The Colliers moved to Riske Creek in 1960, but Eric did not have many years left to enjoy an easier way of life. He died in 1966. Lillian later moved into Williams Lake, and before her death in 1992 travelled extensively. At home she was often asked to give talks on her pioneer days in the Cariboo-Chilcotin, a way of life that has almost disappeared. I am glad their historic "Three Against the Wilderness" home has been preserved. Thank you, Canadian Army Engineers.

*Collier homestead as it looked in 1995 following restoration by Canadian Army Engineers. (Photo courtesy Veasy Collier)*

# More Place Names

In the Cariboo-Chilcotin it seems that just about every place name has a story behind it. Many of the characters and events in these stories have left their name on modern maps. Here is another list of current names and the story behind them.

## Chimney Creek/Lake

There are a number of explanations for how Chimney Creek and Lake got their names, but I believe they were named for a rough stone chimney, all that was left in later years of a priest's cabin (or perhaps a church) built in 1842 at the Indian village near the creek's outlet to the Fraser. Dozens of keekwillie holes (pit houses) can still be seen in the field above the creek.

## Clinton

When the Cariboo Wagon Road was completed in 1863, this settlement previously known as Cut-off Valley and 47 Mile House, was renamed Clinton in honour of Henry Pelham Clinton, fifth Duke of Newcastle, who was the colonial secretary from 1859-64.

## De Sous Creek/Mountain

This appears to be the phonetic spelling of the pioneer name *Dussault* (pronounced "doo soo"). Joseph Dussault was born in Quebec in 1819, later drove oxen on the Cariboo Road, and settled at what became Dussault Creek (De Sous) near the Chilcotin bridge west of Williams Lake.

## Farwell Canyon

Gordon "Mike" Farwell and Gerald Blenkinsop took up land together in the spectacular canyon on the lower Chilcotin River in 1912, and raised horses on their Pothole Ranch. They sold out to the Gang Ranch in 1919, and later the Farwells moved to Victoria.

## Felker Lake

Henry Felker and his wife Antoinette travelled by covered wagon from the U.S., and settled first at the 127 Mile House (first called the Blue Tent) in 1861, then moved to the 144 Mile. Their son Henry Jr. pre-empted land on one of the chain of lakes in the Chimney Creek valley, which was then named for this pioneer family.

## Hat Creek

Originally called *Rivière aux Chapeaux* by early French Canadians who noticed several hat-like depressions in a large rock beside the creek. The rock was later destroyed by road construction. Historic Hat Creek House, established in the 1860s on the original Cariboo Wagon Road beside the creek, is now a B.C. Heritage site.

## Hawks Creek

American-born John F. Hawks came to the Cariboo around the 1860s and went into partnership in a ranch near Soda Creek with John Calbraith, a foreman working on the building of the Cariboo Road. Hawks bought Calbraith out in 1873 and continued with the ranch on his own, calling it Springfield Ranch after his former home in Ohio.

## Horse Lake

On an early map, this lake is designated as *Lac Des Chevaux Noyés 1827*, which translated means Lake of the Drowned Horses. I have no details on the 1827 incident or how the horses drowned, but today the lake is referred to simply as Horse Lake.

## Jones Lake

This small lake south of the 150 Mile House was named for the widow Jones who settled there in 1861. The contractors building the Cariboo Wagon Road got as far as her roadhouse near the 145 Mile when they decided to bypass the first Williams Lake settlement, and instead go by way of Deep Creek to Soda Creek (*Cariboo-Chilcotin, Pioneer People & Places*).

**Macalister**

Named for James H. Macalister who was the first postmaster at this little community which he and his family homesteaded in 1911. Originally from Manitoba, he and his wife Charlotte and five sons were heading for the far North when their team of horses became ill. They stopped just north of McLeese Lake, planted a garden and never left.

**Miocene**

Miocene derived its name from the Miocene gold mine that operated in Harper's Camp, now Horsefly, in the early 1900s. The mine was so named because it was worked in rock laid down during the Miocene epoch. James H. Wiggins was postmaster of the Miocene post office which opened on his Pioneer Ranch in August 1914 and closed November 1969.

**Mitchell River/Lake**

Capt. Josiah E. Mitchell came into the Cariboo in 1861 and in a few short years built a toll bridge across the North Fork of the Quesnel River, cut a trail from 108 Mile to Quesnel Lake, then put boats on the lake to ferry miners and other travellers across.

**Mount Begbie**

Named for Sir Matthew Baillie Begbie, famous judge of gold rush days, it was the highest point (4130 feet) on the old Cariboo Wagon Road. This outstanding landmark near the 83 Mile House has been used for years as a B.C. Forestry lookout station.

**Ochiltree**

The first postmaster of the Ochiltree post office which opened in 1921 near Rose Lake was William Carson Sr. who supplied the name of his birthplace, Ochiltree, Scotland, for the new community. The post office closed June 1957.

**Puntzi Lake**

Originally called Puntzee, the word meant "small lake" in the Carrier Indian language according to a report by Lieut. H. S. Palmer of the Royal Engineers who in 1862 surveyed from the North Bentinck Arm across the Chilcotin to the Fraser River.

*Clinton in 1919.*

### Quesnel

The river and lake were named for Jules Maurice Quesnel, Simon Fraser's lieutenant on his memorable voyage down the Fraser River in 1808. Later, in 1859, the village established at the mouth of the river and the gold rush centre at the junction of the north and south forks (Quesnel and Quesnel Forks, sometimes spelled Quesnelle) adopted the name.

### Timothy Lake

This lake near Lac la Hache is believed to have been named for timothy hay, a fodder grass which grows wild in this area.

### Westwick Lake

Louis Christian Westwick was a hardy Norwegian who came to the Cariboo in 1910, and put down roots in Springhouse. He had his own flour mill, and hauled freight by team and wagon to Ashcroft. He and his wife Myra had ten children.

### Yanks Peak

Bill Luce, an American miner nicknamed the "Live Yank," arrived at the beginning of the Cariboo Gold Rush and staked gold claims on Little Snowshoe Creek above the settlement of Keithley Creek. Luce's cabin became a stopping place on the route to Antler and Williams Creek (Barkerville). He died in 1881 and is believed to have been buried near the peak which bears his name.

# Pioneer Voices

## A Word About the Heritage House
## Pioneer Voices Series

**Western Doctor's Odyssey**. This is the story of Eldon Lee's formative years and his first practice in Hazelton, BC. In an era of corporate medicine and malpractice insurance, Dr. Lee's story is a refreshing reminder of what doctoring is all about. ($11.95)

**Tall in the Saddle** by Eldon and Todd Lee finds two brothers sharing their recollections and observations about growing up on the Hill and Paul Ranch in the Cariboo region of British Columbia. ($14.95)

**Totem Poles and Tea** by Hughina Harold has been called "an adult version of *Anne of Green Gables*" and a "must-read for all BCers" by independent reviewers. It is an enlightening story of a young nurse-teacher's coming of age in a remote 1930s native village. ($17.95)

**Tales of a Pioneer Journalist** by David W. Higgins brings alive 19th century life during the BC gold rush and formative years of Victoria. Higgins, one of the era's most colourful journalists and former Speaker of the BC Legislature, entertains and informs his readers with a style deemed by one reviewer as "un-put-downable." ($16.95)

**Cariboo Cowboy** by Harry Marriott, written in the 1950s, remains the best of campfire reading for horse and nature lovers throughout the west. The ranch setting of Big Bar Lake captures the soul of cowboy life and the dignity of Harry and Peg Marriott. ($14.95)

# More Books on the Cariboo-Chilcotin

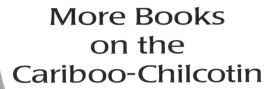

***Godpanning in the Cariboo*** by Charles Hart and Jim Lewis. The first in the Creeks of Gold Series. A detailed guide book designed to help everybody enjoy the beauty of BC's back country while exploring proven gold-bearing creeks long associated with one of the world's great gold rushes. ($9.95)

***Trails to Gold, Volume II*** by Branwen Patenaude. The pioneer roadhouses between Clinton and Barkerville provide us a living heritage of the colourful era of the Cariboo Gold Rush. The trail was ever changing and when the rush was over, the Cariboo-Chilcotin was left with a mosaic of roadhouses and a legacy to build on. ($18.95)

***Chilcotin: Preserving Pioneer Memories*** by the Witte sisters. A vivid text and over 200 photographs recall country extending some 200 miles west from the Fraser River to Anahim Lake. ($39.95)

***Cariboo Gold Rush.*** The saga of 30,000 chasing one of the world's richest discoveries in 1858. They found nuggets by the ton and carved a web of trails and memories into the heart of BC. Maps, photos, bar room tales, success, tragedy and characters galore. ($7.95)

***Wagon Road North*** by Art Downs. One of BC's most popular books with sales over 130,000. Compiled from diaries, journals, eye-witness reports and similar sources. Over 200 photos (16 pages in full color) including St. Saviour's Church, now over 100 years old, and the nearby 1863 graveyard. ($14.95)

# CARIBOO-CHILCOTIN
## Pioneer People
## and Places

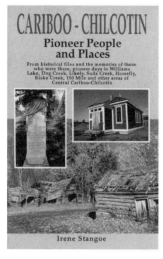

Irene Stangoe's first book was an instant hit in her homeland. Now in its second printing, 28 tales of the past entertain and inform the reader in a folksy style spiced with humour and insight. Stories include:

- ◆ Dog Creek, only the legend survives
- ◆ The Cariboo, how it got its name
- ◆ Pinchbeck—big man in a big country
- ◆ Ghosts aplenty at Soda Creek
- ◆ Cariboo's genuine ghost town
- ◆ The Cowboy and the Princess
- ◆ Forgotten Cariboo-Chilcotin graves
- ◆ Alex Meis and his wooden leg

## About the Author

Irene Stangoe was born in Burnaby, B.C. and has been writing for the *Williams Lake Tribune* for the past 46 years. She and her husband, Clive, bought the newspaper in 1950 and over the next two decades won many awards for their publication, including Best Weekly in Canada in their circulation field.

As well as being community editor and feature writer, Mrs. Stangoe wrote "With Irene," entertaining subscribers with homey stories of kids, dogs and trips to their cabin at nearby Chimney Lake.

After the Stangoes sold their paper in 1973, Irene turned her attention to local history and in 1975 launched a new column for the *Tribune* called "Looking Back," writing of bygone days in the fabled Cariboo-Chilcotin, with special emphasis on Williams Lake.

In 1986 she won first place in the Best Historical Writing Competition sponsored by the B.C. & Yukon Weekly Newspaper Association, and placed second in both 1987 and 1991.

The Stangoes now make their permanent home at Chimney Lake, and continue to write for the *Tribune*.

Visit Heritage House website at http://www.island.net/~herhouse/. For catalogues write Heritage House Publishing Company Ltd at #8-17921-55th Avenue, Surrey, BC V3S 6C4. Please enclose $2.00 for postage. Heritage Books may be ordered through fine bookstores across North America.